Helene Bauer in Vienna

Historical Materialism Book Series

The Historical Materialism Book Series is a major publishing initiative of the radical left. The capitalist crisis of the twenty-first century has been met by a resurgence of interest in critical Marxist theory. At the same time, the publishing institutions committed to Marxism have contracted markedly since the high point of the 1970s. The Historical Materialism Book Series is dedicated to addressing this situation by making available important works of Marxist theory. The aim of the series is to publish important theoretical contributions as the basis for vigorous intellectual debate and exchange on the left.

The peer-reviewed series publishes original monographs, translated texts, and reprints of classics across the bounds of academic disciplinary agendas and across the divisions of the left. The series is particularly concerned to encourage the internationalization of Marxist debate and aims to translate significant studies from beyond the English-speaking world.

For a full list of titles in the Historical Materialism Book Series available in paperback from Haymarket Books, visit: www.haymarketbooks.org/series_collections/1-historical-materialism.

Helene Bauer in Vienna

Political Economy Between Two World Wars

Dunja Larise

Haymarket Books
Chicago, IL

First published in 2025 by Brill Academic Publishers, The Netherlands

Published in paperback in 2026 by
Haymarket Books
P.O. Box 180165
Chicago, IL 60618
773-583-7884
www.haymarketbooks.org

ISBN: 979-8-88890-888-4

Distributed to the trade in the US through Consortium Book Sales and Distribution (www.cbsd.com) and internationally through Ingram Publisher Services International (www.ingramcontent.com).

This book was published with the generous support of Lannan Foundation, Wallace Action Fund, and the Marguerite Casey Foundation.

Special discounts are available for bulk purchases by organizations and institutions. Please call 773-583-7884 or email info@haymarketbooks.org for more information.

Art and design by David Mabb. Cover art is a development from *Construct 21, Kathleen Kersey for Morris & Co. Arbutus / Kasimir Malevich, Fabric Ornament No. 10,* paint and wallpaper on canvas (2005).

Printed in the United States.

Library of Congress Cataloging-in-Publication data is available.

Contents

Preface

In the autumn of 2020 I was chosen to co-lead the project 'Austro-Marxism' for Transform Europe with Walter Baier. Despite my long-standing engagement with state theory, spanning both its liberal and Marxist versions, I realised my limited knowledge of state theory in the Austrian First Republic. While familiar with well-known figures like Joseph Schumpeter, Hans Kelsen, and Otto Bauer, I lacked a profound familiarity with the political theory of Austromarxism compared to its French, American, English, or Italian counterparts. During this time, I delved primarily into the political theories of Antonio Gramsci and Louis Althusser, considered significant representatives of Western Marxist traditions.

Taking over the coordination of the 'Austro-Marxism' project, I immersed myself intensely in the original works of Austromarxism for several years, almost turning this engagement into an obsession. A forgotten world of interwar Vienna unfolded before my eyes, revealing increasing parallels to the present as I delved deeper. This era was marked by deep economic crises, disillusionment with parliamentary democracy, growing societal polarisation, and a profound institutional crisis. The questions then posed by the intellectual circle around the Austrian Social Democracy and the answers they sought are, in many respects, the questions our current society grapples with. Simultaneously, a world of political and economic theory unfolded before me, unparalleled in the twentieth century. The question of why this theory was nearly completely forgotten, particularly in the post-World War II era, finds its answer.

The newly formed party arising from the ruins of the pre-war Social Democratic Workers' Party of Austria, the SPÖ, found itself in a vastly different geopolitical situation than its predecessor. The Cold War era required Austria to carefully position itself as a neutral buffer zone between East and West, significantly influencing the priorities of the Social Democrats. Added to this were a hesitant denazification process and the fact that the outstanding intellectual world of interwar Vienna was completely obliterated during the 11 years of fascist and Nazi terror. The most significant figures of that golden era were either expelled or murdered. The new Austria of the Second Republic was ready to reconcile with its liberal heritage of the interwar period but not with Austromarxism.

Interest in Austromarxism experienced a brief resurgence in the context of the Eurocommunism debates of the 1970s but disappeared after the early 1980s and the rise of global neoliberalism. Since the late 1980s, neoliberal paradigms dominated almost all areas of Austrian social sciences. Although isolated Marxist-inspired research was conducted, it remained without significant resonance. During my time as a student, I was fortunate to encounter professors and underpaid lecturers who opened up a world beyond neoliberal orthodoxy. Without them, this book would not have been possible.

The global collapse of financial institutions in 2008 shook the neoliberal hegemony for the first time, reviving interest in unorthodox economics and political science among some European academics. While the neoliberal hegemony was not shattered, the crisis revealed cracks in its theoretical structure. The time was ripe for alternative political and economic ideas that could encourage us to think beyond global capitalism amidst escalating crises of inequality, debt, growing populism, and flaring conflicts.

Hence, this book about Helene Bauer, a brilliant theorist who always stood in the shadow of her significant husband Otto Bauer. I wrote this book not only because of Helene Bauer's exceptional position in her time but, more importantly, to give a voice back to a brilliant theorist, one of the outstanding figures among Austromarxists. Her analyses often surpassed those of her colleagues from both liberal, conservative, and Austromarxist camps of her time providing many relevant questions and inspiring answers for today's society.

Finally, I would like to express my gratitude to Transform Europe with its director Barbara Steiner and Walter Baier, the city of Vienna, the Rosa Luxemburg Foundation, as well as the Zukunftsfonds of the Republic of Austria, who made this work possible. I would like to thank the Verein für Geschichte der Arbeiterbewegung (Association for the History of the Workers' Movement) in Vienna and especially Georg Spitaler for his willing assistance in the search for Helene Bauer's archival materials. I would also like to thank Vishnu Bachani, whose generous help enabled me to trace Helene Bauer's days in U.S. exile and to find her last text. My thanks go to Sebastian Budgen and Danny Hayward for their commitment to this book, as well as to my editors. Of course, I take full responsibility for any errors that may have been made. Dunja Larise Vienna: November 2023.

PART 1

Helene Bauer: Life and Thought

∵

CHAPTER 1

The Remarkable Life of Helene Bauer

Helene Bauer stands as a notable representative of the Austromarxist movement, an intellectual milieu shaped by Austrian intellectuals in close alignment with Austria's Social Democratic Workers' Party during the latter decades of the nineteenth and early-twentieth centuries. The core ambition of Austromarxism was to usher in a novel socialist society through democratic means. In pursuit of this goal, they consciously distanced themselves from the conventional tenets of Marxism, as well as the doctrines of Bolshevism, eventually diverging from the dogmatic principles of the Third International. Otto Bauer, the celebrated figure of this ideological current and Helene Bauer's spouse, elucidated their stance in the succinct treatise entitled 'Bolshevism or Social Democracy'.[1] Prominent female figures have played a pivotal role in molding the theoretical framework of Austromarxism, making substantial contributions to its intellectual depth and intricacy. Unfortunately, the writings of Käthe Leichter, Therese Schlesinger, Adelheid Popp, Marie Jahoda, and Helene Bauer remain relatively obscure within the global academic community.

Helene Bauer, originally born as Helene Gumplowicz in Kraków on 13 March 1871, hailed from an intellectually oriented family. Her father, Felix Gumplowicz, owned a lending library, and her uncle Ludwig Gumplowicz was a professor of sociology at the University of Graz. Growing up in this environment, Helene was exposed to a multilingual upbringing and developed a penchant for reading books in Polish, German, and French at a young age. Interestingly, she initially failed the entrance exam for the teacher training college due to a perceived lack of musicality, a fortuitous turn of events that paved the way for her unconventional journey into the field of economics – a highly unorthodox choice for a woman during that era. Given the limitations placed on women regarding the study of political science and economics in the Austrian Monarchy, Helene decided to embark on a journey to Zurich to pursue her academic interests. During her journey, she encountered Max Landau in Vienna, and the two eventually married in 1895. Remarkably, Helene did not discontinue her studies due to her marriage, breaking with the norms of her time.

In 1905, Max Landau established a law firm in Vienna, while Helene continued her academic pursuits. In 1906, she completed her doctoral studies in polit-

1 O. Bauer 1920.

ical science and economics at the University of Zurich, successfully defending a thesis on the 'Development of Commodity Trade in Austria'.[2] Following her successful completion of doctoral studies in she authored an 'Outline of the National Economy' in Polish and published it immediately after. In 1908, she contributed to the discourse with another publication in Polish, titled 'The Politics of the Trade Unions'. Throughout this period, Helene managed to balance her academic pursuits with her family responsibilities, having given birth to four children – two daughters and two sons. However, her family life was marked by tragedy, with the loss of her young daughter and the untimely deaths of both sons. Her son Leszek met his tragic end during the battle on the Vistula in 1920, a conflict during the war of the young Polish Republic against the Soviet Union. The second son, Vladek, was a respected statistician and national economist in Warsaw but also passed away at a relatively young age in 1933 due to kidney disease. In 1932, Otto Bauer accompanied Helene on a visit to Poland to see Vladek one last time. Helene Bauer's daughter, Wanda, was an economist as well, and during the First Republic, she resided in Vienna with close ties to her mother. Later, she immigrated to Sweden during the Hitler era but returned to Vienna, where she lived until her passing in 1980.

The Landau's Viennese apartment served as a vibrant hub for socialist intellectual gatherings during that era. It attracted notable figures from both Polish and Austrian social democrats, including individuals like Diamand and Daszynski from Poland, as well as prominent Austrian left-wing intellectuals like Karl Renner, Rudolf Hilferding, and Otto Bauer, who would later become Helene's second husband. The apartment's salon was a gathering place for stimulating discussions and exchanges of ideas. The Café Central in Vienna was another prominent location frequented by left-wing intellectuals of the time. In addition to Austrian intellectuals, the café was known to host individuals like Leo Trotsky and Vladimir I. Lenin for a period, and Helene Landau was among the regular patrons. In 1911, Max Landau decided to relocate his family to Lemberg in Galicia (Lviv in present-day Ukraine), a decision that didn't sit well with Helene. Consequently, she divorced her husband in 1914 and returned to Vienna, where she promptly married Otto Bauer. Otto Bauer was a rising star in Austria's Social Democratic Workers' Party and was a decade younger than Helene. She began publishing under the name Helene Bauer after their marriage. Shortly after their wedding, Otto Bauer was conscripted into World War I and became a prisoner of war in Russia. During this period, Helene aligned herself with the opposition left led by Friedrich Adler, a notable figure in Austrian

2 Landau 1906.

socialist circles. Notably, Friedrich Adler was scheduled to meet Helene Bauer for lunch on the same day he assassinated Prime Minister Graf Stürgkh.

Following World War I, Helene Bauer published her inaugural critical essay in Vienna titled 'On Self-determination of Labour' (*Selbstbestimmung der Arbeit*). This essay was featured in the Viennese social-democratic journal *Der Kampf*. In 1924, she assumed the role of editor at the same journal, working alongside Julius Braunthal and Oscar Pollak. Helene continued to contribute to *Der Kampf*, where most of her treatises were published, until she was compelled to go into exile in 1934. Between 1926 and 1934, Helene Bauer also took on a teaching position in statistics at the Vienna Workers' College. Over a span of 17 years, she penned numerous articles, with the majority appearing in journals like *Der Kampf* and *Arbeit und Wirtschaft*, the prominent journal of Austrian syndicalism. Despite the high quality of her theoretical contributions, these texts have never been reprinted in German, contributing to their relative obscurity in subsequent years.

Helene Bauer's marriage to Otto Bauer was extraordinary for their era. He was a decade younger than her and had already established himself as the most prominent intellectual among the Austromarxists. A close friend of the couple, Otto Leicher, described their marriage as 'a complete spiritual and, above all, intellectual partnership'. Helene played a significant role in helping Otto navigate his relationships with others, especially some of his political colleagues. It was not uncommon for Bauer to inquire, upon returning to their apartment in Kasernengasse, which is now named after him, whether his wife was at home. 'If she wasn't there, he called in the coffee house where Helene was usually staying and asked her to come home. He needed someone to talk to. Helene gave him such rich opportunities for an intensive exchange of ideas that he did not feel the need to lead an intensive social life with friends or political colleagues. Helene, who had brought a penchant for sociability and intellectual discussions from her Galician-Polish family and from her first marriage, tried again and again – often against the resistance of her overworked husband – to gather an intellectual circle in their home. Hans Kelsen, one of the few of Bauer's classmates with whom he was on first-name terms, was a stimulating guest on such afternoons'.[3] Otto Leicher, as well as his wife, economist and social scientist Käthe Leichter, were among the leading intellectuals of Austromarxism. Käthe Leichter was brutally murdered by the National Socialist regime in the Ravensbruck concentration camp, whereas Otto Leichter and their children were able to flee to the United States.

---

3 Leicher 1970, p. 24.

Helene Bauer was a multifaceted figure, deeply engaged in both socialist activism and the field of social science. She actively participated in various debates led by the Austromarxists of her era. Her written works spanned a wide range of topics, including the socialisation of large industries and taxation, where she collaborated with her colleague Käthe Leichter in 1919. She also delved into analyses of the Polish economy and society, writing in both German and Polish. While Helene Bauer engaged in discussions about feminist issues, her primary focus remained political economy. Bauer researched extensively and published prolifically within that field. She held positions of influence, such as being a member of the Vienna City School Board, and played a significant role in shaping educational programs at the Workers' Education Centre. Additionally, she founded the Socialist Workers' Association for Economics and Politics (SAWUP) and led Marxist discussions within it, contributing to the education of a generation of socialist students. Helene Bauer's dedication extended to teaching statistics at the Workers University in Döbling, Vienna. In 1930, she took part in a major research project on women's professional labour in Austria, the *Handbook of Women's Labour*, led by Käthe Leichter. This initiative featured contributions from prominent feminists and female scholars in Austria, and Helene Bauer authored a chapter on 'Women's Labor and Demographic Policy'. Her contributions in these areas showcase her versatile and impactful career in the worlds of activism and social science.[4]

She addressed issues such as the tangible economic challenges that arose subsequent to World War I and the utterly devastating circumstances that remained for the nation following the Great War. She also addressed the planned socialisation of large industries after the Austrian revolution in 1919. After assuming power in Vienna in 1919 and leading the government, the Austromarxists had big plans for the city and eventually the entire country. They were simultaneously engaged in diplomatic efforts to secure the emergence of the Republic of Austria from the ashes of the defeated Austrian Empire at the Peace Conference in Paris. On the domestic front, they had to contend with the hardships resulting from the aftermath of the lost war within their own borders. The fate of Austria hung in the balance, with the possibilities of the country either being divided between neighboring states or emerging as a sovereign nation both equally viable scenarios. This complex and uncertain period in Austria's history set the stage for many of Helene Bauer's writings and political engagements. The strength of the Austrian Social-Democrat Worker's Party, led by Karl Renner and Otto Bauer, as well as the fear of a possible unification

4 Steiner 1997, p. 92.

with Germany, played a crucial role in persuading France and England to grant Austria the opportunity to establish itself as a sovereign Republic. This diplomatic achievement was not without challenges on the domestic front, where the party faced opposition from various quarters.

At home, the Austrian Social-Democratic Worker's Party had to contend with resistance from old monarchists, rural populations who felt that their limited agricultural resources were being depleted by the urban population of Vienna, and the bourgeois upper class who feared potential taxation by the Socialist government to improve the living and working conditions of the poor. The party also had to address the dire economic and social consequences of Austria's defeat in World War I, which included famine, disrupted agricultural supply chains, and the return of unemployed and hungry soldiers. One of the critical issues faced by the Republic of Austria was the loss of agricultural lands that had previously supplied Vienna. These lands were now outside Austria's control, leading to the looming threat of famine. Karl Renner and Otto Bauer pressed their case in Paris, emphasising the urgent need for Austria to regain control over the region of Burgenland, which had been occupied by Hungary in 1918. They argued that without Burgenland, Austria's survival as a state was at risk. This diplomatic effort was instrumental in securing Austria's place as a sovereign republic in the post-war era.

The Austromarxists, while best known today for their extensive housing projects known as '*Gemeindebauten*', had far-reaching ambitions beyond this initiative. During their relatively brief period in power, they introduced a series of progressive reforms that, while having since become widely accepted, were revolutionary for salaried workers in the former Austrian-Hungarian Empire. These reforms included implementing the eight-hour working day, establishing mandatory health and retirement insurance, granting workers a free day each week (Sunday), providing paid vacation, and extending universal suffrage to women. These changes represented a significant departure from the conditions that workers had endured during the empire's era. However, the Austromarxists aspired to achieve even more. They sought to transform key industries from private ownership to social property, a process they referred to as the socialisation of major industries. Additionally, they aimed to socialise investment banks and major industrial enterprises. Their ambition was to create a more equitable economic system but they encountered significant opposition, both from domestic big capital and foreign financial interests. Austria, heavily reliant on foreign credit to rebuild its post-war economy, faced resistance from powerful domestic and international financial forces. These opposing interests thwarted the Austromarxists' efforts to carry out full socialisation. Helene Bauer and her colleague, the economist Käthe Leichter, wrote extensively on the benefits of socialisation for the Austrian people. After the effort to implement socialisation failed, they explored the challenges faced by sovereign states in their efforts to independently manage their economies within the framework of the global capitalist system, highlighting the limitations of national policymaking in a globalised economy.

Helene Bauer played an active role in shaping economic and political debates in interwar Vienna, extending her influence beyond the confines of the Austromarxist movement. One of the main targets of her engagement was the Austrian School of Economics and its prominent thinkers, including Ludwig von Mises, Friedrich von Hayek, and Josef Schumpeter. The concepts formulated by the Austrian School of Economics have become deeply embedded in contemporary culture, often taken as self-evident. These ideas include the belief that the state should refrain from interfering in markets, as it's believed that unfettered markets will naturally lead to optimal economic and social outcomes. The Austrian School also advocates for private entrepreneurship in sectors such as business, banking, industry, health, and education, asserting that these areas should not be subject to public democratic decision-making. These ideas, often characterised as neoliberalism, have become widely accepted today. These concepts were not new and were actively developed in Vienna by the Austrian School of Economics during the 1920s. At that time, they held a dominant position in economic thought. These ideas continue to exert influence in the present day. However, the deregulation of the financial sector in the 1920s, which was championed by neoclassical economics, ultimately led to the catastrophic stock market crash of 1929. Despite the prevalence of these ideas, neoclassical economics could not provide effective solutions to address the subsequent Great Depression that gripped the entire capitalist world for nearly eight years.

The solution to the Great Depression came with the advent of Keynesianism, championed by the economist John Maynard Keynes and becoming the economic program of the U.S. President Franklin D. Roosevelt. This approach involved leveraging public debt to fund extensive public works projects, which led to increased employment and consumer spending, ultimately bringing an end to the Great Depression. The Keynesian policies implemented in the United States under Roosevelt provided a blueprint for successfully combating economic downturns. In Europe, the consequences of the Great Depression were even more devastating, leading to the rise of fascism and national socialism. Helene Bauer was one of the earliest critics of the Austrian School of Economics and their ideas. The neoclassical theories developed by figures like Mises and Hayek saw a resurgence during the neoliberal revolution, notably during the Reagan and Thatcher administrations in the early 1980s. The debates between Helene Bauer and the Austrian School of Economics in the 1920s and early 1930s remain highly relevant today. However, while the works of Mises and Hayek have been widely translated and republished, Helene Bauer's articles have not received any attention and remain unavailable to English-speaking audiences. This has contributed to her ideas falling into oblivion.

Helene Bauer was also engaged in debates with conservative economists such as Ottmar Spann, whose teleological economic ideas she strongly rejected. Ottmar Spann, like Ludwig Mises, established a circle of students and adherents who gathered in their exclusive seminars. Many members of Spann's circle were also part of the Association for the Social Sciences (Sozialwissenschaftlicher Verein), which aimed to promote Spann's state concept. This state concept formed the basis for the Austrofascist authoritarian corporatist state. The activities of the association extended to mobilising against Austromarxism and establishing connections with National Socialists, Christian Socials, and their paramilitary organisation, the 'Heimwehr'. Spann's close political connections with the conservative political elites allowed him to facilitate academic careers for many of his supporters, thereby furthering his fascist political theories.[5]

Helene Bauer engaged in debates with various socialist colleagues and intellectuals, covering a range of topics including money, imperialism, property levy, the future of capitalism, labour theory of value, social economy, and Marxism. Her discussions included prominent figures like Otto Neurath, Fritz Sternberg, Rudolf Goldscheid, Henryk Grossmann, Gustav Cassel, Franz Oppenheimer, and more. During these debates, she demonstrated a dialectical approach to Marxist theory. She viewed Marxism not as a rigid, pre-made instruction sheet but as a flexible framework for analysing evolving situations in the present and future. She developed a scientific methodology for the social sciences based on this adaptable approach.

In the early thirties, particularly following the Great Crash of 1929 and the subsequent depression, Helene Bauer shifted her focus to the global economy and its impact on Austria and Europe. She highlighted the significant political and social power shifts in Europe caused by the Great Depression and linked them to the rise of fascism. She also continued to address issues related to the Polish economy and society and she engaged in discussions about women's emancipation.

In 1934, Helene and Otto Bauer were forced into exile, initially moving to Brno. Subsequently, in 1938, they relocated to Paris, where Otto Bauer passed

5 Olechowski 2014, p. 739.

away due to a heart attack. In 1939, Helene joined her daughter Wanda in exile in Sweden and eventually immigrated to Berkeley, California in 1941 out of fear that Hitler might extend his control into Sweden. Her friends, including the familly Heinzen, Ernst Winkler, Alexander Gerszenkorn, Hans Kelsen, and Gullick, invited her to go to Berkeley, California, as mentioned by her daughter, Wanda Lanzer.[6]

Helene Bauer's last full-length article was published in *Der Kampf* in 1936. This article was one of the early analyses of the fascist economy written in the 1930s, outside of Italy. She continued to write concise reports on the global economy in *Der Kampf*. The headquarters of the publication relocated from Vienna to Brno in 1934, adopting the new name *Der sozialistische Kampf*. In 1938, the publication moved again, this time to Paris, and became *Der Kampf – La lute socialiste*. The final edition of the journal was released on 10 June 1940, just 12 days before the Armistice of Compiègne, which marked the capitulation of France. Following her move to Berkeley, California, Helene Bauer contributed a comprehensive article on the prospective course of socialism to Robotnik Polsky, a Polish socialist journal published in New York.[7]

Helene Bauer passed away in Berkeley on 20 November 1942. In her final days in the United States, she experienced a significant change in her lifestyle. Bauer, who had always been a part of social gatherings and discussions, found herself living in a quiet small town, far removed from the bustling social and political life she had known. She noted that the neighborhood was so peaceful that even dogs didn't dare to bark too loudly. On the evening before her passing, she engaged in discussions about politics with her former Viennese students. Despite the challenges she faced, her answers to questions about the pressing issues of the time were calm and well-considered. Helene Bauer did not live to witness the victory over Hitler's Germany, but by the end of 1942, she already saw the initial signs of victory on the horizon. A few days before her death, she remarked to her students, 'How interesting is life! I want to live another thousand years to see how things turn out'.[8]

---

6 Lanzer 1950.

7 'Despite her age, Helene Bauer remained engaged in the daily global affairs, diligently investigating events and committing her non-conventional opinions to paper. In the New York-based 'Robotnik', she painted a new portrait of socialist Europe. While she observed the politics of Soviet Russia with suspicion and offered sharp criticism, she maintained an unequivocally positive stance toward the economic transformation in Soviet Russia. She had the privilege of witnessing the heroic resistance of the Red Army and catching at least a faint glimpse of a silver lining on the horizon of world history'. Robinson, 1942.

8 Winkler 1967, p. 99.

CHAPTER 2

Turbulent History of the First Austrian Republic and Austrian Social Democracy

Understanding the historical context of the period between World War I and Hitler's annexation of Austria is crucial for appreciating the significance of Austrian social democratic politics during that time. This was a tumultuous era marked by significant political, social, and economic changes. The First Austrian Republic emerged from the ashes of the Austro-Hungarian Empire after World War I, and the leaders faced numerous challenges in the post-war period.

The demise of the Austro-Hungarian Empire and the birth of the nascent Austrian Republic marked a process that commenced on 3 October 1918, culminating in the formal proclamation of the Republic of Austria on 12 November 1918. This transformative trajectory was instigated by the pressing imperative to halt the devastating war in which Austria and Germany found themselves, a war they were on the precipice of losing. Their aim was to forge a peace accord that would stave off the spectre of an imminent and complete defeat. Emperor Karl, the final Habsburg monarch, proved unable to secure a separate peace agreement for Austria with the Entente powers. Consequently, it fell to the representatives of the Social Democratic Worker's Party (SDWP) in the State Council of the Empire to seize the initiative, thereby effecting the cessation of both the war and the Austro-Hungarian Empire. Crucially, the SDWP had already affirmed the principle of self-determination for nations during their Party Congress in Brno, an ideal that gained additional traction through the concurrent advocacy of U.S. President Woodrow Wilson. On 3 October 1918, Victor Adler, the prominent leader of the left-wing faction within the Social Democratic Worker's Party (SDWP) and a distinguished member of the Empire State Council, made a resounding proclamation. He emphasised the pressing necessity of halting the ongoing war and initiating the formation of a new German-Austrian state. In keeping with their staunch commitment to the principle of national self-determination, Adler acknowledged the rightful aspirations of the Slavic peoples to forge their own national entities. Simultaneously, he championed this same right for the German-speaking population of the Austro-Hungarian Empire. Adler's perspective stood in stark contrast to the monarchists, who clung to the delusion that the Empire could somehow withstand the impending defeat in the Great War. Victor Adler, with prescient clarity, recognised that in order to shield the heartland of Austrian territory from potential division among the victorious Entente powers, swift action was imperative, necessitating the establishment of a new nation-state.

In the Council, two additional political parties, namely the German National Party (GNP) and the Christian Social Party (CSP), found themselves without independent proposals and thus opted to align themselves with the lead taken by the Social Democratic Worker's Party (SDWP). Acknowledging the pressing urgency for action, they jointly issued a memorandum on 9 October. Their spokesperson, Viktor Kleinböck, who would later serve as the Minister of Finances in the inaugural republican government, represented their collective stance. Emperor Karl, though not inclined to abdicate outright, confronted the unanimous consensus of all governing parties. Under this weight of unity, he signed a rather nebulous manifest on 16 October. This declaration articulated Austria's transformation into a federal state wherein each federal unit would possess the prerogative to forge its own state. Simultaneously, the council engaged in deliberations concerning the fundamental character and territorial boundaries of the emerging Austrian state. Ambiguities still shrouded whether the forthcoming state would adopt a republican or monarchical form, if it was to be a monarchy, and whether it wwould entail the continued reign of the Habsburg dynasty or the ascendancy of another royal house.

In terms of delineating borders, the plan exhibited a degree of wishful thinking, as it seemed to be more an expression of aspirations than a reflection of the complex realities of wartime and diplomatic negotiations. The primary aim was to incorporate the Sudeten German region in Bohemia, a territory over which the Czech Republic also asserted its claim, and to safeguard South Tyrol. South Tyrol had been militarily annexed by Italy, which had laid claim to it as early as 1915, as a condition for entering World War I on the side of the Entente. Then, on 21 October 1918, the three political parties arrived at a consensus to establish the new 'German-Austrian state'. At this juncture, two pivotal issues remained unresolved: whether the state should adopt a republican or monarchical form, and whether the ultimate goal was to unite this new state with Germany. The Social Democratic Workers' Party (SDAP) advocated for the establishment of a republic and the unification with Germany. In contrast, the monarchists and the Catholic factions were opposed to both propositions, while the Communists opposed the idea of unification with Germany.

Within the Socialist camp, Otto Bauer emerged as the most vocal proponent of unification with Germany. It might initially appear paradoxical that Socialists, on the cusp of dismantling the monarchy and founding a republic, would advocate for unification with Germany. However, Otto Bauer's rationale was rooted in the belief that aligning with Germany would facilitate a smoother transition to socialism, given the considerable influence wielded by German social democracy. Moreover, at that juncture, the notion of an Austrian nation was still in its nascent stages. Austrian nation building had only just commenced and it is essential to recognise that, in contrast to many historical precedents where nation building precedes state building, the Austrian case unfolded differently. The process of Austrian nation building proved protracted, spanning three decades and marked by numerous setbacks before reaching its culmination. It is evident in hindsight that the full realisation of Austrian nation building transpired only with the establishment of the Second Republic following World War II. In 1918, both options, whether Austria would unite with Germany or chart an independent course, were equally plausible. The determining factor in the trajectory of Austrian sovereignty was not solely the preference of the Austrian populace but, rather, the reluctance of the Entente powers to permit the amalgamation of Austria with Germany.

Otto Bauer's fervor for unification with Germany was so pronounced that he chose to withdraw from the peace negotiations in Saint Germain when it became clear that the Entente powers would not entertain the idea of unification under any circumstances. His decision to withdraw was driven by a desire to avoid becoming a hindrance, given his well-known advocacy for unification. It's important to note that his support for unification was not primarily rooted in German nationalism or imperialism. Instead, the rationale articulated by Otto Bauer and Max Adler stemmed from a concern that a 'crippled Austria' might not be able to survive independently, let alone attain the goals of socialism. They were convinced that the realisation of socialism necessitated integration into a more expansive economic sphere. Conversely, the German Social Democrats displayed less enthusiasm for the potential unification with Austria. Their reservations were grounded in concerns about potential territorial losses in both the East and West of Germany if the Entente permitted the annexation of Austria. They also harbored doubts about whether such unification would be conducive to the socialist revolution in Germany. Overall, the diminishment of Austria into what was pejoratively referred to as a 'postage-stamp-principality' (*Zwergstaat*) proved a bitter pill for most cosmopolitan and educated socialist intellectuals and politicians to swallow. This sentiment was palpable in a letter addressed to Karl Kautsky, underscoring Otto Bauer's resignation: 'If the union is not implemented, Austria will become a poor peasant state, where politics will not be worth the effort'.[1]

On 25 October 1918, while Emperor Karl was still the reigning monarch, he appointed Heinrich Lammasch, an individual previously uninvolved in polit-

1 O. Bauer 1995, p. 477.

ics, as the last prime minister of the Austro-Hungarian monarchy. However, this government's tenure would prove exceedingly brief. During this time, Czechs, Slovaks, Slovenians, and Croatians officially aligned themselves with the newly established Slavic states, while the Austrian population held onto the hope that, in accordance with Woodrow Wilson's doctrine of self-determination, they too would be permitted to forge their own German-Austrian state. On 30 October 1918, representatives from the three most influential political parties came to a sober realisation: Austria's fate rested in the hands of Woodrow Wilson. Given Wilson's reputation as a champion of Slavic independence, the delegates of the Social Democrats, German Nationals, and Christian Socials sent a letter to Wilson, beseeching him to endorse the creation of an Austrian Republic. In taking this step, they effectively asserted their authority to represent Austria on the international stage, rendering the Lammasch Government de facto obsolete. On the same day, 30 October 1918, these three parties established both a provisional National Assembly and State Council, which assumed the governing responsibilities. The State Council comprised the three presidents of the National Assembly and an additional 20 members. It was this State Council that appointed Karl Renner as the head of the government, and he remained in office until 15 March 1919. Since Emperor Karl played no active role in these developments, this effectively constituted the proclamation of the Austrian Republic. Finally, on 12 November 1918, the Republic was officially declared from the Austrian Parliament building.

On the day of the official proclamation of the Republic, the streets of Vienna swelled with crowds who had congregated in front of the parliament building on the Viennese Ring. They enthusiastically brandished the new red-white-red flags of the Republic. Nonetheless, the ceremony was not without its share of controversy. Emperor Karl had abdicated the day before, and the monarchists no longer obstructed the path to the formation of the new Republic. However, the recently established Communist Party of Austria (KPÖ) held a different vision for the new state. They believed that the nation should transcend mere republicanism and embrace communism. The KPÖ was founded on 30 November1918, and swiftly emerged as a rival to the Social Democratic Workers' Party (SDAP) in the quest for the favour and votes of the Viennese working class. Like other prominent political forces in Austria, the Communists maintained their own paramilitary organisation known as the 'Red Guard'. This militia was primarily composed of disillusioned and embittered former members of the Imperial army who had returned from the front lines.

During the ceremonial speech delivered by the new Prime Minister Karl Renner, a group of Communists assembled in front of the Parliament and made an attempt to stage a coup, pressing to breach the building. They also seized control of the editorial offices of the *Neue Freie Presse* press agency, coercing the editors to publish a special edition of the newspaper that adhered to their directives. While the Social Democratic Workers' Party (SDAP) was a Marxist party, in contrast to the Communists, their political aspirations were grounded in a pragmatic understanding of the international power dynamics shaping Europe's future. Karl Renner, known for his pragmatism, advocated pursuing the socialist cause through cooperation within the framework of a coalition state that included the bourgeoisie. Even Otto Bauer, positioned on the left wing of Social Democracy, exhibited a keen awareness of the unique Austrian and European circumstances. The Austromarxists recognised the impracticality of applying the Bolshevik strategy of revolutionary state overthrow, followed by the establishment of a Communist Soviet, to Western Europe. This viewpoint was shared by the renowned Italian communist Antonio Gramsci, who maintained that a revolutionary overthrow could only succeed under the most favourable conditions in less developed states lacking a robust bourgeoisie and advanced state structures. In the Western states characterised by complex power dynamics and bargaining mechanisms inherent in advanced capitalism, such an overthrow would likely result in bloodshed and failure. Another crucial factor influencing the resolute rejection of a Communist revolution by the Austromarxists was the dire situation in which Austria found itself in November 1918.

Indeed, following its defeat in World War I, Austria found itself bereft of a functioning army and was further constrained by prohibitions against raising one. This left the country vulnerable to potential invasion by the victorious armies of the Entente powers. In this context, a Communist uprising held the potential to undermine the legitimacy of the newly established government, casting it as ineffective in the vital task of state building. Moreover, such a revolt could have imperiled the very existence of the fledgling Republic.

During the early days of November 1918, the new Austrian state was far from being a geopolitical certainty. The government faced an arduous struggle to safeguard the Republic from being dismantled by the neighboring nationalist aspirations. A successful Communist coup could have spelled the demise of any prospects for forming a cohesive Austrian state, and the Austromarxists within the Social Democratic Workers' Party (SDAP) were acutely conscious of this critical reality.

Having been defeated, Austria had no army anymore and was even prohibited from raising one and defending itself from an eventual invasion by the Entente's victorious armies. A Communist uprising would have undermined the legitimacy of the newly established government, making it appear incapable of the state-building function. It would also have put the newly established

Republic in peril. During early November 1918, the new Austrian state was not a geostrategic certainty; the new government was to fight with all means to secure the new Republic from being dismembered by the neighbouring nationalist pretension. A successful Communist coup could have annihilated every possibility of building an Austrian state, and Austromarxists of the SDAP were deeply aware of that.

Following its defeat in World War I, Austria found itself bereft of a functioning army and was further constrained by prohibitions against raising one. This left the country vulnerable to potential invasion by the victorious armies of the Entente powers. In this context, a Communist uprising held the potential to undermine the legitimacy of the newly established government, casting it as ineffective in the vital task of state-building. Moreover, such a revolt could have imperiled the very existence of the fledgling Republic. During the early days of November 1918, the new Austrian state was far from being a geopolitical certainty. The government faced an arduous struggle to safeguard the Republic from being dismantled by the neighboring nationalist aspirations. A successful Communist coup could have spelled the demise of any prospects for forming a cohesive Austrian state, and the Austromarxists within the Social Democratic Workers' Party (SDAP) were acutely conscious of this critical reality.

As observed by historian Hans Hauptman, the Socialists' argument that, in the event of a proletarian dictatorship, the Entente powers would permit Austria to suffer from food shortages resonated strongly among the working-class population. This perspective held more sway than the counterargument put forth by the Communists, who claimed that 'Soviet Hungary will provide us with food'. In hindsight, the subsequent defeat of the Hungarian Communist Soviet under Béla Kun and the Bavarian Council Republic in 1919 confirmed the Socialists' suspicions and validated their cautious approach. In response to the initial shots fired on the parliament by the Communist 'Red Guard', Karl Renner called for the intervention of the Volkswehr. This 'Volkswehr' was a provisional military unit organised by Julius Deutsch, a member of the Social Democratic Workers' Party (SDWP) and secretary for military affairs. Deutsch recognised the imperative for the new Austrian Republic to have an armed force and thus assembled an ad hoc provisional military unit comprising 16,000 to 17,000 personnel. Initially, the force operated under the authority of the soldiers' councils rather than the officers. Over time, the Volkswehr transformed into a state military under the allegiance of the Christian Social Government, and the Social Democrats progressively lost their influence over it.

The transition from the Austro-Hungarian Monarchy to the Austrian Republic is a subject that has sparked differing opinions among both contemporaries and historians. The classification of this event as a revolution or as a natural outcome in the power vacuum is a matter of debate. In traditional terms, a revolution often implies a violent and abrupt overthrow of one political system in favour of another, as witnessed in the French or Russian revolutions. However, in the case of Austria's transformation, there was an absence of widespread bloodshed, and the monarchy's leadership, particularly Emperor Karl, did not meet a fate similar to the beheadings seen in more conventional revolutions. The shift from the monarchic system to a republican one unfolded progressively and relatively peacefully, making it feel unlike a revolution to many of its contemporaries. Austromarxists and some legal scholars like Hans Kelsen, who authored the Austrian Constitution, viewed this transition not as a political revolution but as a legal one. According to Kelsen, the change was a juridical transformation. The new 'Renner Constitution' of 30 October 1918, represented a radical departure from the old imperial constitution, marking the abolition of the Habsburg dynasty, the aristocracy, and the previous authoritarian military structures and ushering in a republican democratic framework. For Otto Bauer, who devoted an entire book to the Austrian Revolution, it was not a proletarian revolution akin to the Russian Revolution of 1917. Instead, he characterised it as a national bourgeois revolution catalysed by Austria's defeat in the Great War.

Ultimately, the categorisation of this historical transition as a revolution or as a more gradual evolution remains a subject of scholarly discussion and interpretation.[2] The Austrian Social Democrats played a pivotal role in shaping the trajectory of the Austrian Revolution, steering it away from a full-fledged proletarian revolution in the style of the Bolsheviks. This pragmatic approach focused on state building and stability, with an emphasis on preventing a more radical transformation. The sentiment expressed in the leading Viennese newspaper on 12 November 1918, reflected a similar understanding of the revolution: 'Non-bloody revolution created German Austria, without barricades and without the Bastille'.[3] For Walter Baier, 'The victory of the bourgeois revolution was not won on the barricades by the insurgent people, but fell into their lap through the defeat of the Habsburgs in war'.[4]

Upon assuming office, the new Renner Government was immediately confronted with challenges that posed a threat to the newly established Republic. Not only were the hopes of reclaiming South Tyrol from Italy and the Sudeten areas in Bohemia from Czechoslovakia dashed during the peace conference in Saint Germain, but the core territories of Austria were also vulnerable, facing the risk of annexation by neighboring states. The region now known as

2 O. Bauer 2021.

3 *Neue Freie Presse* 1918.

4 Baier 2021, p. 19.

Burgenland was historically considered part of West Hungary by the Imperial authorities, and the newly formed Hungarian state asserted its claim to this territory. The Austrian delegation vehemently contended that this land was indispensable to Vienna's survival, primarily due to its role as an agricultural hinterland. Hungary had occupied this area and was reluctant to relinquish it. It was only through U.S. mediation that a resolution was reached, with Austria gaining control of the territory subject to a referendum in the city of Sopron, which ultimately chose to remain in Hungary. In the southern parts of Austria, King Alexander of Serbia, who had expanded his dominion in World War I to encompass Bosnia and Herzegovina, Croatia, and Slovenia (now referred to as the Kingdom of Serbs, Croats, and Slovenians), harbored ambitions to annex Styria and Carinthia. He launched an invasion into these regions. The peace treaty of Saint Germain imposed a prohibition on the defeated powers from raising arms against the Entente members, even in the case of an invasion. In defiance of this prohibition, the German Austrian 'Heimwehr', the paramilitary force associated with the Christian Socials and the German Nationals in Carinthia and Styria, chose to fight back to protect these territories.

A settlement was ultimately brokered with the assistance of the United States. Once more, a plebiscite was conducted to determine the fate of the two provinces, and it was decided that they would not be divided and instead remain within Austria. The 'Heimwehr', initially established in 1918 for the defense of the southern borders, transformed and evolved into an anti-socialist militia that represented the interests of big capital and conservative factions. This shift in the Heimwehr's objectives led to confrontations with the organised workers' movement and played a pivotal role in undermining Austrian democracy. It set the stage for the rise of Austrofascist forces to power in 1934, marking a significant turning point in Austria's political landscape and history. The integration of Austria into the new Republic was a process marked by significant challenges, even within the core regions of the country. Historically, Austrian provinces tended to be highly conservative, holding anti-socialist and anti-Semitic sentiments. Moreover, the majority of people in these regions often viewed Vienna as a 'Socialist-Jewish' centre of power, perceiving it as a place that siphoned their agricultural products to sustain what they considered its 'lazy' population. The requisitions necessitated to address the famine that erupted in the winter of 1918–19 in Vienna only served to exacerbate these tensions.

In this climate, Vorarlberg made a petition and held a referendum in 1919, seeking to join Switzerland. The referendum received strong support, with 80 percent of the population favouring annexation to Switzerland, an action justified by reference to Woodrow Wilson's doctrine of self-determination.

However, the Entente powers voted against this move, highlighting the precedence their geopolitical interests took over the perceived right to self-determination. A similar situation unfolded in what is now Lower Austria, which sought to unilaterally join Germany. The Constitution of 1920, which established a decentralised federal structure, gradually alleviated the tensions between the various Austrian states and Vienna. This constitutional arrangement represented a compromise between the Socialists, who favoured a centralised state to facilitate the implementation of social rights, and the anti-socialist regionalism of the periphery, which was represented by the Christian Socials. In contrast to the Weimar Republic's constitution, the Austrian Social Democrats failed to incorporate social rights into the Constitution of Austria, reflecting the broader challenges and divisions that characterised the country during this period.

This episode represented one of the early setbacks for the Social Democrats in their dealings with the conservative Austrian hinterland. The prevalent atmosphere of strong anti-Semitism and anti-socialism, combined with the lack of a unified Austrian national identity that transcended regional and German affiliations, was vividly illustrated in an anonymous letter. This letter, authored by an individual identifying themselves as 'Karnute', was published in the *Grazer Tagesblatt* in July 1919.

The sane mind of the German alpine man shrugs off the destructive spirit of the Semites, who want to rule the Republic of German-Austria from the water head-Vienna and, in the interest of other races, prevent any organic reorganisation ... we reject any dictatorship, which thoroughly Jewish Vienna imposes on us with all determination ... And if the Soviet Republic should really be set up in Vienna to the cheer of Israel and its international borders, then there would probably only be one answer from our free mountains, and that would be the immediate proclamation of the Alpine Republic, which would once and for all initiate the clean separation and give us full freedom of action in relation to the Socialist-Communist big-city desperadoes.[5]

The Christian Social Party played a significant role in intensifying these sentiments, even within Vienna itself. The chief editor of the Worker's journal (*Arbeiterzeitung*) perceived this campaign against Vienna as a form of aversion directed toward the capital, which had now fallen into economic hardship. Those who had previously benefited from Vienna's status as a thriving centre of commerce were now less inclined to show solidarity with the city during its moments of crisis.[6]

---

5 Karnute 1919.

6 Austerlitz 1919.

In just a matter of weeks after coming into power, the Social Democrats government in Austria introduced a series of groundbreaking legislative changes. These included granting women the right to vote, implementing an eight-hour workday, and establishing state unemployment compensation. Within a few months, they also passed laws that introduced factory councils, paid vacations, and initiated the socialisation of large economic enterprises. The socialisation of major industries, a process that involved compensating private owners through a wealth tax, was envisioned as a step toward achieving democratic socialism. According to Otto Bauer, democratic socialism entailed 'the economic self-management of the people'. Otto Bauer took on the role of heading the newly established State Socialisation Commission to oversee this ambitious plan, which aimed to facilitate a peaceful transition to socialism. However, this grand vision faced staunch opposition from the bourgeoisie and the wealthy elites. Otto Bauer attributed the failure of the socialisation plan to the fact that Austria had been prevented from uniting with Germany and that the Workers Movement was primarily strong in Vienna, while the rest of the country remained deeply conservative and anti-Socialist. Käthe Leichter, another member of the Socialisation Commission, offered a more nuanced analysis of the socialisation project and its shortcomings in her article titled 'Experiences of the Austrian Socialisation Experiments'. She highlighted the insurmountable challenges inherent in attempting to socialise major industries within a system where the financial sector and creditor banks remained in private hands.[7]

The post-war economy posed the most pressing challenge for the new government, with a host of contributing factors converging to create a crisis for the newly established state. However, the most detrimental factor was the nation's near-complete dependence on foreign capital. Austria's situation was exacerbated by a failed war effort, a devastated economy, and an increasing reliance on imports, as the country had contracted and lost access to its previous supply chains. The war left Austria burdened with a significant budget deficit and an industry that was reluctant to recover. In addition, the return of thousands of soldiers to Austria seeking employment and income further strained the nation's resources. Historian Karl Stadler aptly described the situation, with foreign capital treating Austria as if it were a colony, reflecting the country's precarious economic position. 'The Germans neglected the Styrian iron and steel industry in favour of the Ruhr, and Austria's large oil deposits around Zistersdorf were not exploited by their western owners for similar reasons. If

7 Steiner 1997. The original text translated in English will be available soon in Historical Materialism series.

there were good times in Austria, then it was a sham economy, as a result of inflation, speculation or the occupation of the Ruhr by the French'.[8]

The post-war inflation took a heavy toll on the unemployed, and the meagre wages of those still employed lost value with each passing day. However, it's worth noting that inflation did offer some benefits to certain Austrian industries, as their products became more competitively priced on the international market. In an attempt to stimulate domestic industries, import taxes were introduced throughout Europe. Unfortunately for Austria, this further limited its export opportunities, resulting in a substantial trade deficit that reached billions. By 1923, the trade deficit had swelled to 1.15 billion Schilling, underscoring the severe economic challenges the country faced in the aftermath of the war.[9] The consequence of the economic turmoil was a rapid increase in unemployment. To exacerbate the crisis, the League of Nations imposed stringent conditions on Austria's access to credit. Ignaz Seipel, the Christian Social prime minister, traveled to Geneva on 4 October 1922, to negotiate a new line of credit for the reorganisation of Austria's economy. He agreed to these credit conditions, which included further reductions in salaries and social security benefits that had been initially implemented by the Renner Government. Additional taxes on goods and services were also mandated, and the League of Nations appointed a General Commissioner to oversee the implementation of the fiscal austerity measures outlined in the Protocol. This arrangement effectively rendered Austria entirely reliant on foreign creditors, deepening the country's economic dependence on external sources during a challenging period.

The conditions set by international capital banks for extending credit to states in the early-twentieth century bear a striking resemblance to the conditions seen in contemporary times. This similarity is not surprising, as both eras were influenced by the same economic principles that continue to inform global financial strategies today, particularly following the global neoliberal revolution that gained momentum in the 1980s. As in more recent times, creditors imposed austerity measures on Austria as a precondition for their credit, mirroring the austerity measures enforced on Greece following the 2008 financial crisis. These measures entailed severe cuts to the social benefits system, including areas such as unemployment and medical security, retirement security, public education, and childcare. These social benefits had been introduced in 1918 by the Socialist Renner Government as a means to achieve budget stability and a strong currency. However, a fundamental problem with such aus-

8 Stadler 1968, p. 229.

9 Weissensteiner 1990.

terity strategies, both then and today, is that they tend to reduce economic output, exacerbate unemployment, and limit consumption. Rather than using credit to invest in production and innovative technologies that could enhance production efficiency, increase employment, and subsequently stimulate both spending and economic growth, austerity policies tend to intensify dependence, undermine the real economy, render loan repayment increasingly difficult, and extinguish prospects for long-term economic recovery. This same strategy, which has led to persistently growing deficits in Greece and other European debtor nations in the twenty-first century, was employed in Austria during the early 1920s, illustrating the enduring and problematic nature of such economic and financial approaches.

Austerity, as practiced in Austria during the 1920s, did not resolve the economic downturn; instead, it exacerbated the situation by stifling innovation, production, and consumer spending. This approach trapped Austria in a vicious cycle of borrowing and servicing debts, perpetuating its economic struggles. Helene Bauer highlighted this as a primary argument against the Vienna School of National Economics in the 1920s, a school of thought that was considered one of the most influential advocates of such an economic program. These perilous economic ideas experienced a revival during the governments of Ronald Reagan and Margaret Thatcher in the 1980s and have since become the dominant economic doctrines of global capitalism in the twenty-first century. They have influenced the strategies of institutions like the European Central Bank (ECB) and the Troika when managing deficits in countries such as Italy, Spain, Portugal, and Greece. Furthermore, the Austrian investment banks in the 1920s engaged in credit and debt speculation, a practice similar to what contemporary European banks did (and continue to do) in the decade leading up to the global financial crisis of 2008. Out of the 370 banks operating in Austria in 1923, 100 went bankrupt due to speculative activities. Much like the banks in more recent times, these insolvent Austrian investment banks sought massive bailouts from the state in 1923. While the bailouts were provided, the outcome, then as now, was a significant budget deficit. Unfortunately, this deficit was addressed through austerity measures rather than investments in production and technology, a pattern that has endured over time.

In a manner reminiscent of contemporary neoliberalism, the capital of that era sought to transfer the burden of the crisis onto the working class, rather than accepting a reduction in its own profits. Despite being below pre-war levels, workers' wages were deemed excessive and social benefits such as medical and unemployment insurance, retirement insurance, public education, and public housing were targeted for reduction. Notably, the Social Democrats of Red Vienna did not finance the construction of public apartments through credit. Instead, they funded public housing by taxing the wealthy. This approach was viewed as a more significant affront to the affluent elites than the emergence of a budget deficit. During their time in government, the Social Democrats introduced taxes on capital, luxury goods, real estate, and servants, which elicited outrage among the upper classes. The economist Ludwig Mises from the Austrian School of National Economics and the philosophers Ottmar Spann and Ernst Jünger were among the intellectual figures at the forefront of the opposition to taxing the rich. Helene Bauer engaged in polemics with these figures, often demonstrating brilliance and humor in her arguments. With the democracy in Austria during the early 1920s, the working majority gained political empowerment. In response, the upper classes increasingly supported antidemocratic and authoritarian tendencies as a means to preserve their privileges, which they believed were threatened by the majority vote when democracy affected their economic interests.

Starting in 1920, the Christian Social Party gained significant political strength, while the Social Democratic Workers' Party (SDWP) remained in opposition until the end of the First Republic in 1934. The Christian Socials' rise to power was underpinned by robust voter support in the provinces, the backing of the Catholic Church, and, even more crucially, their close alignment with the interests of big capital. This alliance encompassed the Central Association of Industrials, banks, creditors, landowners, and trade, among others. Once in power, they exerted their influence over the state bureaucracy, the military, and the police by appointing their own loyal cadre. They also maintained control over the 'Volkswehr' and frequently employed the 'Heimwehr' militia, consisting of conservative peasants, ex-military officers, entrepreneurs, wealthy rentiers, and former aristocrats. However, the parties representing the interests of salaried workers retained a solid voter base and had strong professional associations, such as the Workers Chamber, which was established as a counterpart to the Chamber of Industry and Commerce. In contrast to today, the working majority still had the ability to resist, to some extent, the attempts by the capitalist classes to shift the burden of economic crises onto workers by reducing salaries and social benefits while safeguarding capital gains. This ability to resist such measures left the wealthy elites dissatisfied with democracy. The SDAP recognised that the rich elites were prepared to discard democracy when their privileges were threatened by majority rule, replacing it with fascism in an effort to preserve their interests.[10] In 1924, the SDAP formed its own militia called the 'Republikanischer Schutzbund' to counterbalance the con-

10 Linzer Program 1926, III/2.

servative militias. This move aimed to defend democracy against authoritarian pressures. However, the SDAP found it challenging to offer salaried workers the protection they expected from their parliamentary representatives in dealing with the crisis. As a result, dissatisfaction with liberal democracy, which failed to secure social rights, began to emerge among the working classes. This disillusionment with liberal democracy led to a shift among the masses toward more authoritarian political options, a process resembling what we now refer to as populism.

The strategy employed by the 'Heimwehr', which was furnished with weapons by Italy and Hungary, was to provoke street confrontations with the workers, unleash a sense of tyranny, and result in the loss of life and injury.[11] The objective was to instill a sense of fear and then offer protection and safety. The situation came to a head in 1927 when violent clashes erupted, culminating in the arson of the Ministry of Justice building. The Heimwehr, a conservative paramilitary organisation, launched an attack on an SDWP demonstration, resulting in a tragic outcome with 84 demonstrators and five police officers losing their lives. While many of the fatalities were attributed to conservative militias, some were arrested but later released by the court. In response, the SDAP organised a massive protest in front of the Palace of Justice, decrying the court's rulings. The police, the Volkswehr, and the Heimwehr met the demonstration with brutal suppression and the enraged crowds set fire to the Palace of Justice. Increasingly cognisant of the weaknesses within the organised workers' movement, conservative forces pushed for more authoritarian rule. They achieved this by enacting various emergency decrees, which they portrayed as necessary for restoring order. This marked the beginning of a gradual erosion of democracy by conservative elites. The SDAP was hesitant to deploy its militia, the 'Republikanischer Schutzbund', for fear of triggering a full-blown civil war. The path toward fascist dictatorship was carefully orchestrated, taking into account the Social Democrats' reluctance to engage in a protracted civil conflict.

Amidst this already volatile situation, Austria and the world were shaken by the events on 24 October 1929 (known as Black Thursday) when the New York Stock Exchange crashed. This event triggered one of the most extensive economic crises and recessions ever witnessed in the capitalist world. Production credits were severely constrained, and despite the counsel of renowned economist John Maynard Keynes, the United States continued to pressure Germany and Austria to fulfill their post-World War I reparation obligations, further destabilising these two nations. These pressures led to an escalating

11 Simon 1984, p. 114.

budget deficit, high unemployment rates, and rampant inflation. By 1931, the crisis had reached its zenith in Austria. The Creditanstalt, Austria's largest bank and a key creditor for the Austrian industrial sector, defaulted on a debt of one billion Schilling. The Austrian state was once again compelled to step in as the lender of last resort. This exacerbated both the currency crisis and the existing budget deficit. Unemployment rates surged to 15.4 percent in 1931, 21.7 percent in 1932, and eventually peaked at 25.5 percent in 1934.[12] The plan to create a tariff union with Germany to ease the exports failed on the resistance of France, who feared it would pave the way for Austrian unification with Germany, which was indeed on the table in this deal. 'The German monopoly capital wanted to pave the way for the annexation of Austria to Germany through a customs union using financial and economic policy measures'.[13] As the prospects for a union with Germany dwindled, the idea of forming a confederation with fascist Italy and Hungary began to gain appeal.[14]

In June 1931, the SDAP received a coalition proposal from Ignaz Seipel (CS), who was once again tasked with forming a government. The SDAP rejected this proposal. Otto Bauer, who was positioned on the left wing of the party, offered the following explanation for the rejection: 'It should be declared that the party, aware of the state's difficulties, is ready to take part and is also ready to support any government, but the condition for the Social Democrats to enter the government is a complete change of political and economic course'.[15] Karl Renner, who was on the pragmatic (sometimes even called right) wing of the party, rejected this proposal as well: 'If we had a loyal party, like 'Das Zentrum' in Germany, we might dare to enter the government, but we won't do that with our bourgeois parties, for the simple reason that we won't allow that the guilt of the regime for these twelve years, this whole moral, political and economic collapse, is then passed on to social democracy in the end'.[16]

For some historians, this decision marked a pivotal moment in the history of Austrian Social Democracy. By rejecting the opportunity to share power, they

---

12 Bihl 1989, p. 474.

13 West 1957, p. 49.

14 Otto Bauer didn't object to the state bailout for Credit Anstalt, recognizing the potential catastrophic consequences its failure could have on the Austrian economy, including increased recession and unemployment. However, he insisted that the bailout should be conditional on the state taking over Credit Anstalt. This perspective on bailouts, with a condition of public ownership, resonates with some contemporary radical left movements in Europe, especially regarding the bailouts provided to bankrupt banks in the aftermath of the 2008 financial crisis.

15 O. Bauer 1931, p. 2.

16 Renner 1931, p. 58.

missed a chance to influence the course of events. For others, who took a more realistic view, they believed that the Austrian Social Democracy, as a junior partner in a coalition with the Christian Socials, would not have the strength to enact the significant changes needed at that time. They feared that the SDAP would be complicit in policies they were too weak to redirect in a more favourable direction, as Karl Renner had predicted.

The approach taken to address the rampant budget deficit during this period involved austerity policies rather than Keynesian deficit-financed, state-backed infrastructure and industrial projects. Unlike the approach taken in the United States by Franklin D. Roosevelt to boost consumption and create employment, which embraced Keynesian principles, both the Christian Socialists and Social Democrats in Austria pursued austerity policies. The Christian Socialists were influenced by the Neoclassical School of Economics, particularly represented by the Austrian School of Economics. They saw austerity as a means to stabilise the economy. On the other hand, the Austromarxists supported austerity because of their adherence to Marxian theories of value and their fear of hyperinflation. Their shift toward Keynesianism occurred too late to salvage the situation, as their credibility in economic matters was already weakened.

It's worth noting that Helene Bauer, in contrast to Otto Bauer and Rudolf Hilferding, did not support austerity policies as a remedy to economic crises. Otto Bauer recognised the need for state intervention but was uncertain about the specifics of what was required. Keynes' theories, which argued for a more interventionist role of the state in managing the economy, were later validated by history. However, it's important to note that when these events occurred in the early 1930s, Keynes had not yet published his influential 1936 work 'The General Theory of Employment, Interest, and Money', which would shape future economic policy.

The consequences of the economic crisis in Austria had severe political ramifications. As the austerity measures now also affected the state administration (a traditional voter base of the Christian Social Party) many of those affected turned to support the National Socialists, the Austrian counterpart to the Nazi Party in Germany. The continued strength of the workers' parties and associations in Austria, which prevented the complete transfer of the financial burden onto the working classes, contributed to the rise of fascist tendencies among the Christian Socials. This was further fueled by support from Mussolini's Italy. In this politically charged atmosphere, a conflict between the Socialist and Conservative factions in the parliament led to the formal blockade of the Parliament on 4 March 1933. Seizing this opportunity, the government under Engelbert Dollfuß announced its intention to govern by decree. Additionally, on 16 March 1933, the Dollfuß government introduced anti-terror legislation, providing a legal basis for banning demonstrations and conducting raids against members and associations affiliated with the SDAP (Social Democratic Workers' Party) that were suspected of engaging in loosely defined 'terrorist activities'. Demonstrations that were held despite the ban were brutally suppressed, and the National Council was suspended. These actions marked a significant shift toward authoritarian rule in Austria.

The Christian Social Party disbanded and became a Patriotic Front, which also included members of the Volkswehr and Heimwehr. The leaders of the SDAP remained reticent about deploying military force, despite the emergence of a fully-fledged fascist regime. They announced a general strike, but didn't act on it. The critical turning point came in February 1934 when a raid against the SDAP headquarters in Linz led to spontaneous clashes with workers, spreading to Vienna. Unfortunately, the 'Republikanischer Schutzbund' (Republican Defense League), an armed workers' organisation, was unprepared for the confrontation, and only a small contingent reached Vienna in time to join the battle. The lack of well-coordinated armed resistance and a general strike contributed to the defeat of the workers' movement. The defeat of the workers marked the end of Austromarxism. Subsequently, the SDAP, its affiliated trade unions, and its cultural and sports associations were banned, and the Vienna City administration, which had been democratically elected, was removed from office. The events resulted in hundreds of lives lost, nine Social Democratic leaders executed, and hundreds more imprisoned. On 1 May 1934, a new fascist constitution was decreed, officially beginning the Austrofascist dictatorship. This marked a tragic end to the democratic and socialist hopes that had characterised the early years of the First Austrian Republic.

After the violent clashes and defeat in February 1934, the subsequent ban of the SDAP and the persecution of its members, Helene and Otto Bauer sought refuge in Prague. Most of the party's grassroots supporters turned to the now-illegal Communist Party. The Communists quickly became a central force in the active antifascist resistance against the emerging Austrofascist regime. In addition to the Communist movement, some former SDAP members organised a new underground party they called the Revolutionary Socialists. This was a response to the ban on their original party and an attempt to continue the struggle against the fascist regime. Confronted with a disaster, Otto Bauer took responsibility for the debacle of the February uprisings. 'We avoided the fight because we wanted to spare the country the catastrophe of a bloody civil war. The civil war broke out eleven months later, but under much less favourable conditions for us'. He admitted errors in his strategy, but maintained that other socialist or Communist European strategies could not prevent the rise of fascism either.

The Hungarian Social Democracy in 1919, and the Italian Social Democracy up to 1922, pursued a left-wing, revolutionary policy akin to Communism: it ended in catastrophe in both countries. On the other hand, German Social Democracy has chosen a very statesmanlike, very national, very right path: it also has been defeated. In Austria, we tried to take a middle path between the Italian-Hungarian and the German extremes – we were also defeated. The causes of the defeats of the working class obviously lie deeper than in the tactics of the parties, obviously deeper than in individual tactical mistakes.[17]

The leading Austrian Communist intellectual, Ernst Wimmer, commented on what for him appeared as fatalism: 'Otto Bauer was sublimely able to present every past defeat as inevitable and do the same in terms of the future, prophesying inevitable victories'.[18] Historian Fritz Weber saw the main reason for the collapse of Social Democracy in their incorrect economic approach during the crisis, in which they supported the government's austerity politics instead of offering Keynesian solutions.[19] According to Julius Braunthal, the hesitation in organising armed resistance was due to Otto Bauer's pacifist disposition. 'The truth about Otto Bauer is probably that nature had not meant him to be leader of battles ... This feature of human gentleness in Bauer's nature, which ennobled his personality, is admittedly a character trait of weakness when it comes to brutal power struggles'.[20]

However, unlike German Social Democracy, the Austrian didn't go down in silence. It was defeated in an armed confrontation. Otto Bauer's words that the defeat of the Austrian Social Democracy opened the way to Hitler's eastward expansion paving a way toward the next devastating European war turned out to be prophetic. 'Europe will yet experience what a key factor in European peace was destroyed with Austrian Social Democracy'.[21]

17 O. Bauer 2021, p. 74.
18 Wimmer 1981, p. 323.
19 Weber 1986, p. 4.
20 Braunthal 1961, p. 83.
21 O. Bauer 2021, p. 30.

CHAPTER 3

Helene Bauer and Austrian School of Economics – On Methodology and Bias in Economics

Can there be a 'bourgeois' and a 'socialist' doctrine within the scope of economic theory, if it is limited to ascertaining the purely empirical facts and conceptually processing their connections, without one being necessarily wrong if the other is correct? Of course, different answers are possible to the question 'how should the economy be' depending on the political, social, ethical point of view of the one who gives the answer; but can there be opposite answers to the question 'how is the economy' that are not based on a lack of knowledge or on wrong conclusions and yet seem to be mutually exclusive?[1]

Methodological individualism, a prevailing approach in contemporary economics, finds its historical origins in the intellectual milieu of interwar Vienna. Pioneered by Alfred Schütz and Felix Kaufman, this methodology became an integral component of the intellectual discourse among third-generation marginal utility theorists, with a central orbit around Friedrich Hayek's 'Mind circle' and Ludwig Mises' 'Privatseminar'. Notably, both Hayek and Mises owe a significant debt to Alfred Schütz, a renowned Viennese philosopher of social sciences who immigrated to New York in 1939. Schütz employed the framework of marginal utility theory as an exemplar of how 'ideal-typical' constructs facilitate the generation of objective and universally applicable judgments. His methodological treatises in the realm of social sciences were profoundly influenced by the philosophical tenets of Edmund Husserl and his transcendental philosophy. According to him, social phenomena (including economic relations) were not to be understood through the lens of the empirical social sciences and factual analysis, but rather 'according to the essential invariant structures of a soul or a community of spiritual life: that means according to their a priori'.[2]

The foregoing passages suggest that methodological individualism presupposes an inherent, immutable, and historically invariant core of human nature. Within the economic writings of Mises, Hayek, and their adherents, this con-

1 Bauer 1925, p. 63.
2 Schütz 1932, pp. 41–2.

cept evolved into that of the 'isolated economic agent' (*isolierter Wirt*), serving as the fundamental unit of reference in their analyses of social and economic phenomena. Conversely, as articulated within the intellectual milieu of Austromarxism, the framework for social sciences, of which economics constituted a pivotal component viewed the individual subject as a social construct. In this perspective, both the subject's social and economic conduct and its subjectivity were understood as products of their (historical) interactions with the society they coexisted with and actively co-created. Consequently, Austromarxists formulated their methodology without resorting to metaphysical conjecture or invoking notions of a universally applicable, eternal, or a priori human nature. Instead, they embraced a method grounded in meticulous empirical observation. Paul Lazarsfeld, a member of the intellectual circle of Austromarxism, together with his wife Marie Jahoda, who later assumed a professorship in social sciences at the University of Sussex, emerged as a prominent figure in advocating for the positivist empirical approach to social sciences in the United States. His efforts led to the establishment of the Bureau of Applied Social Research at Columbia University.

These two schools of thought engaged in a competition centred on the ideals of 'scientific precision' and 'objectivity', with each side leveling accusations of ideology, bias, and unscientific methods against the other. Ludwig Mises staunchly adhered to the theory of self-evident a priori judgments, a concept influenced by Schütz, but he tempered it to some degree by shedding some of the Husserlian phenomenological intricacies. In his view, a priori reasoning served as the methodological cornerstone for a non-empirical social science he termed praxeology:

> Praxeology is a theoretical and systematic, not a historical, science. Its scope is human action as such, irrespective of all environmental, accidental, and individual circumstances of the concrete acts. Its cognition is purely formal and general without reference to the material content and the particular features of the actual case. It aims at knowledge valid for all instances in which the conditions exactly correspond to those implied in its assumptions and inferences. Its statements and propositions are not derived from experience. They are, like those of logic and mathematics, a priori. They are not subject to verification or falsification on the ground of experience and facts.[3]

---

3 Mises 1998, p. 32.

The critique that this approach to social sciences lacked scientific rigor and was fundamentally inadequate for a comprehensive understanding of social phenomena was not solely the purview of Austromarxists. Indeed, while they were among the early proponents of this viewpoint, they were not alone in their contention. The initial clash between apriorism and empiricism dates back to the 1870s, involving key figures like Carl Menger, the first-generation economist of the Austrian School, and the leadership of the New Historical School, notably Gustav von Schmoller. The latter group rejected a priori assumptions while still embracing abstract theoretical constructs, which, in their view, had to be firmly grounded in empirical knowledge and factual evidence. On the other hand, Menger was not as unwaveringly committed to a priori thinking as Mises, but his methodological stance was essentialist with a particular emphasis on the central role of analytical reasoning in economic theory. This theoretical clash also had a significant institutional dimension, as it coincided with a struggle for supremacy within academic institutions. This intellectual conflict, referred to in the history of economics as the '*Methodenstreit*', exerted a far-reaching influence not only on the Socialist calculation debate but also on prominent figures such as Alfred Marshall and the Cambridge School.

Otto Bauer expressed his appreciation for his teacher, Carl Grünberg, for his adept use of the methodology of the German Historical School and its fusion with Marx's historical framework. In Bauer's view, this integration served as a counterbalance to the prevailing dominance of the 'pure' theory associated with Carl Menger and the Austrian School. It also offered a remedy to what he perceived as 'the peril of exclusively relying on abstract concepts, which, at best, can aid in the analysis of empirical data but cannot supplant the need for the direct study of that material'. It's worth noting that even within the Austrian School, profound disagreements on this matter persisted, with Friedrich Hayek adopting a stance opposite to Mises.

With the ascendance of Keynesianism and the establishment of scientific positivism at American universities, Mises was increasingly regarded as an unscientific economist. Mises's student, economic historian Bruce Caldwell wrote of his scientific methods: 'Professor von Mises has a splendid analytical mind and an admirable passion for liberty, but as a student of *human nature* he is worse than null and as a debater, he is of *Hyde Park* standard'.[4] Even Friedrich Hayek, expressed reservations about Mises's apriorism after Mises's death, saying he 'never could accept the … almost eighteenth-century rationalism in his argument'.[5]

---

4 Caldwell 2004, pp. 125–6.

5 Hayek 1978, p. 137; Hayek 1994, pp. 72–3.

Nevertheless, the underlying concept of abstract, self-evident, a priori, and essential individuality that characterised early neoliberalism continues to persist in the contemporary neoliberal paradigm. In the present context, it takes the form of the fictitious selfish individual endowed with rational judgment and possessing adequate information concerning matters of self-interest. This individual serves as a foundational reference point for rational choice and public choice theories.

The marginal utility theory, rooted in methodological individualism, and the Marxist theory of economics, grounded in dialectical and historical materialism, presented diametrically opposed conceptions of the social world and human subjectivity. This dichotomy gave rise to two conflicting approaches for analysing social phenomena. In reference to Helene Bauer's quote at the outset of this passage, these theories were considered 'mutually exclusive'. Acceptance of one implied the other must rest on either erroneous conclusions or misguided assumptions. Consequently, the debate between the Austrian School of Economics and Austromarxist economists transcended the discussion of contemporary social and economic issues, serving as a direct confrontation between these fundamentally contrasting visions of society.

For Helene Bauer, every economic exchange, which is the very foundation of the economy, has a distinctly social character. This stands in stark contrast with the concept of the 'isolated economic agent' and the abstract individuality of the marginal utility theory for 'it 'contrasts' the individual, the 'isolated economic agent' – detached from the community and thus historically indeterminable – with a given supply of goods'.[6]

Helene Bauer criticised neoclassical economists for what she saw as their outright rejection of the entirety of Marxian social theory, attributing this stance to their focus on the technical aspects of Marx's theories of value. In contrast, she staunchly defended the Marxian labour theory of value, asserting it as the theory elucidating the supply side of the economy. However, it is important to note that she was not blind to the shortcomings associated with the labour theory of value, which originally had roots in the works of Adam Smith and David Ricardo and was subsequently incorporated into Marx's framework. Bauer advocated for an objective measure of value that was intrinsic to the production and exchange process, as opposed to a subjective assessment influenced by demand and market prices. In her view, the latter did not represent the true value of the goods offered for exchange but rather reflected the power relations within the given society. 'The new doctrine seemed to meet all the

6 Bauer 1924, p. 106.

requirements that the bourgeoisie, feeling itself in a defensive position due to social struggles, could impose on a social theory. The self-contained economy oriented towards use-value, in which prices are derived from the value estimates of individuals based on the calculation of value, where the work of social individuals, shaping their existence through technology in their struggle with nature, is dissolved into a condition of existence alongside technology and nature, simultaneously disintegrates human society into loosely related economic subjects'.[7] Helene Bauer was not the first Austromarxist to undertake a critical examination of the Marginal Utility theory. Rudolf Hilferding, an Austromarxist who also served as the Minister of Finance in the Weimar Republic on two occasions, engaged in a debate with Eugen Böhm-Bawerk, a second-generation economist from the Austrian School who held a professorship at the University of Vienna, as early as 1904. It's noteworthy that Ludwig Mises and Otto Bauer were both students of Böhm-Bawerk.

In contrast to Rudolf Hilferding, who staunchly rejected the concept of marginal utility, Otto Bauer, who emerged as one of the foremost economists within the Austromarxist movement, sought to find a middle ground between the labour theory of value and the notion of marginal utility. He stated that

> … the value theory of the marginal utility school has by no means remained meaningless … Until the marginal utility theory introduced a more detailed analysis of changes in demand, one was (…) often of the opinion that the demand was a fixed measure. As a result, the dependence of demand on price was frequently underrated. The fact that the market price is the price at which supply and demand coincide is a discovery of the marginal utility theory. We do not yet find this theory in Marx. This market price theory is related to the marginal utility theory.[8]

Emil Lederer, Walter Schiff, and Alfred Braunthal made efforts to integrate marginal utility theory into Marxian economic theory. Helene Bauer reviewed Emil Lederer's work, 'Outline of Economic Theory'. In her assessment, she contended that the new concepts Lederer aimed to introduce to Marxian economic theory by drawing from marginal utility theory were already encompassed within Marx's examination of the process of price formation.[9] Hans Zeisel, a younger-generation Austromarxist born in 1905, openly voiced his criticism of

7 Bauer 1924, p. 107.
8 O. Bauer 1956, p. 288.
9 Bauer 1925.

the Marxian labour theory of value, characterising it as outdated and inaccurate. He aligned his perspective with the views of the Russian-Polish-German economist Ladislaus von Bortkewitsch.[10]

Helene Bauer did not champion the labour theory as a universal explanatory model for exchange value simply for its own sake. Instead, she observed that neoclassical economics failed to recognise the societal interdependence inherent in value, which she regarded as a fundamental aspect of Marx's social and economic theory. In her perspective, liberal economists seemed to fixate on Marx's 'labour value', primarily scrutinising it to determine if it aligned with observed market prices, seemingly entranced by this aspect. 'They endeavour ... to bury it all together under the mountains of value theoretical disputes, which often replace serious economic research'.[11] Helene Bauer's agenda was not centred on defending the labour theory of value, but rather on emphasising the critical significance of social power relations within the economy and the necessity of incorporating them into the development of an appropriate economic methodology. Well before the emergence of heterodox economics and institutional political economy, Helene Bauer recognised the importance of power dynamics in society and their role in economic theory. Her major achievement in the debate with the Austrian School of Economics lay in underscoring the relevance of these power relations.

This concept would later find resonance with Kurt Rothschild, a second-generation Austromarxist born in 1914. In his influential work, 'Price Theory and Oligopoly' (1947), Rothschild combined a critique of marginalism and game theory, highlighting their limitations in addressing complex economic issues due to their lack of a holistic approach and their failure to grasp the notion that economics is a multifaceted social science where power exerts its influence on every aspect of economic rationality. These ideas were subsequently taken up by Paul Baran and Paul Sweezy in their 1964 book 'Monopoly Capital'. 'The new doctrine now had the task of attributing the social distribution of goods to the same elements of satisfaction, usefulness, and quantity on which the marginal utility theory had been built, to return to the logical connection between the starting point and the individual problems, and thereby conceptually grasp and present wages and profit as natural economic phenomena independent of historical power and dependency relations'.[12]

10 Zeisel, 1930.

11 Bauer 1926, p. 63.

12 Bauer 1924, p. 107.

Another crucial aspect of Helene Bauer's theoretical framework and another point of contention with the Austrian School was her strong advocacy for the synthesis of qualitative and quantitative research methods. She firmly believed that, on their own, quantitative methodswere inadequate for comprehending the full scope of economic relationships. However, this didn't imply that she underestimated their significance as methodological tools in economics. In fact, she even taught statistics at the 'Wiener Arbeiterhochschule Döbling'. Her perspective was rather that quantitative methods were most effective when the categories they were intended to measure had already been delineated and differentiated through prior qualitative analysis. In other words, she saw qualitative analysis as a necessary precursor for ensuring the meaningful application of quantitative techniques in economic research.

To quantitatively determine income types derived from labour, i.e., from a productive function, and all other income types flowing from the ownership title, they must first be qualitatively distinguished, i.e., differentiated in their essential characteristics. However, this means recognising and admitting that their level is not determined by economic factors but by social factors, not by 'productive contributions' but by class power, not by 'performance' but by influence. The bourgeois science of economics cannot not exceed the limits of this knowledge.[13]

Helene Bauer held the view that neoclassical economics was both incapable and disinclined to incorporate social power relations into their analytical framework. She perceived this reluctance as stemming from a pronounced pro-capital bias, if not a deliberate effort to conceal the unequal power relations that arise from a capitalist market economy. The marginal utility of this doctrine, to which it owes its fame and its official position, is conditioned by its 'participation' in the cover-up of social contradictions and by its 'productive contribution' to the defense of the property which it is willed to deliver, even if so it makes an agreement on 'the theory' and on the nature of its main problems and their overall context increasingly difficult. The bourgeoisie can see it as proven with satisfaction that wages are always equal to the income, that is, 'attributable' to the worker and that on top of that 'wage payment is one of the brakes on production, while entrepreneurial profit is not (Schumpeter, 1934)'.[14]

---

13 Bauer 1924, p. 112.

14 Ibid.

1 The Problem of Attribution of Value in the Marginal Utility Theory

Helene Bauer's concerns extended beyond her critique of the Austrian School of Economics for its failure to consider the social determinants of the economy and its resulting individualistic approach to methodology. She also sought to highlight inconsistencies in the associated theory of value. She identified shortcomings in the theories of value attribution presented by proponents of the marginal utility school, including Gustav Cassel, Carl Menger, Friedrich von Wieser, and Eugen Böhm-Bawerk. In particular, Carl Menger raised questions about the quantitative determinability of the value shares attributed to 'goods of the higher order', which encompass individual production factors and their contribution to the value of the final product.

Helene Bauer contended that the attribution issue arose from the necessity of recognising rent as a phenomenon that fundamentally corresponded to the ultimate value, regardless of the influence of social power relations on 'marginal utility value'. Consequently, the proportions of the value associated with labour, land, and means of production should be expressed in terms of the output of the final product, thereby indicating the economic significance of each unit. It is worth noting that both the economists of the Austrian School and Helene Bauer and the Austromarxists intentionally employed different terminology to describe the same economic phenomena, such as 'value', 'labour', and 'land' versus 'goods of different order'. This linguistic distinction underscores their explicit ideological disparities.

Regarding the final product, Friedrich von Wieser introduced a distinction between 'common' attribution, which applies to products made from productive resources with multiple uses, referred to as 'cost-productive means', and 'specific' attribution. In the case of specific attribution, the value of the means of production is derived as a residual amount after subtracting the costs of the productive means from the total revenue.[15] In contrast, Helene Bauer, aligning her perspective with that of Hefendahl and Schumpeter, counters this argument by asserting that the wage rate within the capitalist economy is not determined by the price of the final product. Instead, it is considered a fixed unit established prior to the initiation of the production process.

> The wage, (...), is here not derived from the value of the end product as a cost element, but is assumed as a given quantity already in the production and treated as a cost, the deduction of which reveals the value

15 Mayer 1900, p. 1214.

> shares of the more or less specific factors.[16] They are merely a "... difference between the price of labour and the price of the end product", which, although it provides a correct description of the capitalist distribution method, does not explain it from the logic of economic action as a whole, as Wieser assumes.[17]

Gustav Cassel, one of the leading economists of his time, offered another solution for the attribution of value expressed in the end product's price. In his words: 'This general price-fixing process's social, economic task is, briefly, the realisation of the general economic principle in the exchange economy. The pricing process solves this problem by simultaneously securing the necessary regulation of demand by eliminating the less important wants and the proper direction of production by the fullest and most economical use of all the available factors of production'.[18]

However, according to Helene Bauer, the price formation process in the capitalist barter economy does not deliver on what Cassel claims it does.

Not the 'less important', but the less viable (*kauffähige*) wishes are eliminated because it can be more advantageous for their owners, who are private owners, to withdraw them from the market. Accordingly, production management is not led by general economic (rationality) but by individual purposes. As a result, 'general economic efficiency' converts into a particular capitalist economic efficiency, accompanied by 'rich and poor,' 'poverty and abundance,' and 'boom and decline'.[19]

Helene Bauer's position is that the general necessities of social life assert themselves alongside a free price formation; otherwise, the 'modern exchange economy' could not exist. However, 'they assert themselves in an antagonistic way, which at the same time allows waste and compel to privation'.[20]

Helene Bauer maintained that for an exchange economy to function, a common denominator for all value judgments must be established from the outset. She contended that economic theory should reflect real-life processes. She concluded that the marginal utility theory replaced values with prices and valuations with monetary estimates, ultimately leading to a price theory rather than a value theory.

16 Hefendehl. H., *Das Problem der ökonomischen Zurechnung. Eine kritische Untersuchung der Lehre von der funktionellen Verteilung*, Essen, 1922. Cited as such in: Bauer 1924, p, 109.

17 Bauer 1924, p. 109.

18 Cassel 1967, p. 91.

19 Bauer 1925 A, p. 93.

20 Bauer 1925 A, p. 94.

This contention sparked further debate on the issue of value attribution. Even Joseph Schumpeter, a disciple of the Austrian School of Economics, regarded the theory of value attribution as a weak point in the marginal utility theory. Among all the scholars of the Austrian School, Helene Bauer held Joseph Schumpeter in the highest esteem. She credited him with being the first to thoroughly scrutinise and critique the significant flaws in the attribution theories put forth by his own teachers. Schumpeter's solution was simple and pragmatic. He argued that the productive success of the three categories (labour, capital, and land) is so interdependent that there is no criterion to distinguish which factor of production takes precedence over the others.

Helene Bauer concurred with Schumpeter's deduction, but this held true only if the utility value was accepted as the initial point of departure in the general theory of value. She added that it was also right to claim that the 'utility value of labour equals zero if labour is not used properly or deprived of the conditions to produce! Although both answers are equally correct or incorrect, the economic determinants of capitalist distribution can still not be derived from any of them'.[21]

The production-driven theory of value that Helene Bauer presents as an alternative to a demand-driven theory is not inherently purely rational. Instead, it places a strong emphasis on the concept of fairness in all economic calculations and accords a privileged position to individual or collective labour within the theory of value.

Only labour exchanged for labour now appears as an exchange of equal values of the same kind and therefore comparable at all. This exchange is only possible within the circle of working people who create different goods for each other through their labour, exchanging them directly or indirectly through the mediation of money and the market, which tells each individual whether their individual labour is really useful for others and to what extent. *Those who do not belong to this circle do not possess an equivalent exchange good at all,* cannot have one, because it can *only be acquired through personal dedication.*[22]

2 Against Ludwig Mises' Scientific Apologetics of Privilege

Ludwig Mises vehemently opposed the social policies implemented by the Social Democratic Worker's Party of Austria in the aftermath of the Great War. These policies were a response to the severe economic consequences of the

21 Bauer 1924, pp. 111–12.
22 Bauer 1926, p. 64.

war and the loss of agricultural lands and markets following the dissolution of the Austrian Monarchy. In 1918, Vienna experienced widespread hunger, disease, and extreme destitution. During the '*belle époque*' the city faced enormous housing challenges, as many residents shared beds, essentially sleeping in shifts. Sanitary facilities were commonly shared among tenants, and numerous rooms lacked windows, resulting in limited airflow and sunlight. Despite these harsh living conditions, rents remained high.

The Social Democratic Worker's Party of Austria, which secured a resounding victory in the Vienna elections, implemented a progressive taxation system to finance extensive public housing projects throughout the city. Unlike the typical approach of relying on debt, these public projects were entirely funded by taxes. The party imposed taxes on what were considered luxury goods and services, such as cars, horses, and servants. Even privately owned homes, typically associated with the privileged, were subject to taxation. This period, known as 'Red Vienna', also brought about regulations on working hours and introduced mandatory social, medical, and retirement security measures that were previously unheard of. However, these initiatives aimed at improving living conditions in the city were vehemently criticised by their conservative opponents, with Ludwig Mises being one of the most vocal critics. They viewed these measures as nothing short of 'destructionism' and, at times, even labelled them as 'terrorism'.

Ludwig Mises strongly criticised the social reform policies of 'Red Vienna', asserting that they were built upon a 'terror apparatus'. He rejected the historical link between the widespread hunger in 1918 and the subsequent mass unemployment. Instead, he expressed support for the controversial 'self-protection associations', namely the Wehrbund and Heimbund, which would eventually evolve into the armed forces of Austrofascism and play a pivotal role in the overthrow of liberal democracy in Austria. This aspect of Mises' perspective was often downplayed or overlooked by his liberal admirers in the United States.[23]

From the standpoint of scientific rigor, Mises' criticism of the Red Vienna's social reforms appeared weak and inadequately substantiated. Instead, it was marked by strong partisan fervor and resentment. In his 1922 book '*Die Gemeinwirtschaft*', Mises primarily argued that the public's calls for reforms in Vienna were driven by what he saw as the base envy of the poor toward the rich. He even provided an illustrative case involving a friend who, in Mises' view, justly opposed being taxed for the benefit of public housing projects.[24]

23 Mises 1978, pp. 47–9; pp. 57–9.

24 Mises 1922.

Helene Bauer ironically alludes to Mises's book, suggesting that the concept of happiness derived from fulfilling one's desires appears to be an ethical principle that is reserved solely for Mises's friends, and not for ordinary people and workers. She implies that Mises employs economic arguments to discredit those who still dare to express such desires, seeking to prove them utterly wrong.

The 'natural wages' barriers must not be exceeded, even if they are drawn too narrowly to satisfy the feelings of pleasure. Only evil envy can burst them, and only from the sad fact that 'even today the common man tends to regard the state as a source of rent from which he wants to draw as much income as possible'[25] and that he 'is averse to the unemployed income, as long as someone else receives it and not himself'.[26] So, it is how Mr. Mises explains the dissatisfaction of the common person with the existing state of affairs.[27]

A later conservative commentator, Whittaker Chambers, published a scathing review of the same book in the National Review. In his critique, he contended that Mises's thesis, which suggested that anti-capitalist sentiment was primarily rooted in 'envy', represented a form of 'know-nothing conservatism'.[28]

Helene Bauer was not the first figure from the Left to enter into a debate with the staunchly conservative Ludwig Mises. Karl Polanyi, a renowned socialist sociologist in Vienna during the interwar period, engaged in an extensive and substantive debate with Mises concerning the topic of a socialist economy in the early 1920s. As elaborated in his seminal article *'Die Wirtschaftrechnung im sozialistischen Gemeinwesen'* (its English translation by S. Adler appeared in 1935 in *Collectivist Economic Planning: Critical Studies on the Possibilities of Socialism*, edited by F.A. Hayek), Mises did not believe any socialist economy viable without a direction provided by the prices built within a free market.[29] Polanyi polemically responded with several articles between 1922 and 1924.[30] In early January 1920, at the presentation of the *'Die Wirtschaftrechnung'* at a meeting of 'Nationalökonomische Gesellschaft', Helene Bauer was among the attendees, which included Joseph Schumpeter, Alfred Amonn, and Max Adler. In a letter to Emil Lederer (who did not attend the meeting) dated a day after on 14 January 1920 Mises wrote about the reception of his speech:

25 Mises 1922, p. 61.
26 Ibid.
27 Bauer 1923B, p. 591.
28 Tanenhaus 1997, p. 500.
29 Mises 1920.
30 Polanyi 1922.

My first concern is to show that economic calculation, as it is practiced in the free economy, is inconceivable in a socialist commonwealth because it is built on the premise that money prices are formed for the means of production. This part of my presentation has generally met with full consent in the discussion in the 'Nationalökonomischen Gesellschaft'. Even Max Adler and Helene Bauer have made objections on merely one point, namely, that economic rationality will choose other ways and means in the socialist commonwealth than they will in the free economy. But what these means will be, they could not specify.[31]

Helene Bauer did not engage in a debate over a socialist economy with Ludwig Mises. Instead, her focus was on refuting Mises's portrayal of a liberal, rational, competitive capitalism that was believed to inevitably increase general social wealth – a concept that echoes in the contemporary 'trickle-down economy' thesis. According to Bauer, Mises' sociological perspectives were based on historically fictional premises, promoting the idea of liberal harmony underpinned by utilitarian ethics. She disagreed with Mises' rejection of the connection between capitalist development and the imperialist world war. Bauer observed how Mises depicted himself as a lone voice in what he considered a 'socialist desert' in the context of 'Red Vienna'. He even viewed bourgeois science as under siege from what he perceived as socialist, culture-endangering 'destructionism'.[32]

Ludwig Mises advocated for the political elimination of the labour movement and supported social cutbacks. He viewed efforts to secure legal protections for workers and limit working hours as part of what he termed socialist 'destructionism'. Mises also did not refrain from diminishing social security measures, characterising them as sources of new 'widespread diseases'. In the 1920s, he openly called for a civil war against labour unions and even endorsed fascism as a quick solution to what he saw as the ills of social democracy.

It cannot be denied that Fascism and similar movements aiming at establishing dictatorships are full of the best intentions and that their intervention has, for the moment, saved European civilisation. The merit that fascism has thereby won will live on eternally in history. But though its policy has brought salvation for the moment, it is not of the kind which could promise continued success. Fascism was an emergency makeshift. To view it as something more would be a fatal error.[33]

31 Hülsmann 2007, p. 377.

32 Mises 1925, pp. 266–93.

33 Mises 1927, p. 30.

These well-known and frequently criticised stances exemplify Mises' attitude towards policies aimed at reducing inequality and advancing a more equitable distribution of wealth. They also reveal his readiness to jettison democratic principles in order to protect privilege. In contrast, Helene Bauer maintained a steadfast commitment to democracy and defended it unwaveringly until the end. She passed away in Berkeley, holding onto her confidence in the ultimate triumph over fascism and national socialism.[34]

34 Winkler 1967.

CHAPTER 4

Socialisation

The first administration of the newly established Austrian Republic seized control of a state that had been utterly depleted by the war. In the first year, the Republic received humanitarian assistance from the U.S. government through Italy. Therefore, the foremost objective of the new government was to resuscitate the state's economy. All political parties agreed on the necessity of economic recovery, but they differed on how to achieve it. The first coalition government, a partnership between the Social Democratic Workers' Party (SDAP) and the Christian Socials, featured three key figures playing equal roles in formulating the state's economic revival plan. These were: Otto Bauer, leader of the SDAP, head of the newly established Socialisation Commission, and minister of foreign affairs; Joseph Schumpeter, an eminent economist within the Austrian School and the finance minister of the new Republic; and Karl Renner, who served as the prime minister. This cabinet was the result of a coalition agreement between the SDAP and Christian Socials, with Joseph Schumpeter appointed as a non-party minister by the Christian Socials.

The expectations of the SDAP leaders were established along with their aspirations for unification with Germany and subsequent incorporation into a larger state, with the expectation that this would help establish a socialist system. Schumpeter, however, was an opponent of unification with Germany. He hoped for an economic and trade union with the now sovereign states that made part of the former Austrian Empire in which he expected Vienna to become a major financial and trading centre. It soon became apparent that Austria's destiny was to be a small, but independent country after both hopes were disappointed at the negotiating table in Saint-Germain. In this new reality, the financial and economic survival strategies and long-run revival were to be recalculated from both sides. While these new calculations subsequently began to demonstrate some common features, they also brought to light irreconcilable differences.

Joseph Schumpeter advocated for the primacy of a capitalist economy and the unfettered pursuit of entrepreneurship as the driving forces behind post-war economic recovery and financial stability. While he acknowledged the necessity of economic revival, he remained ambivalent about the specific economic model to adopt. The spectrum ranged from a laissez-faire free market system to a form of state-directed capitalism. In contrast, Otto Bauer championed the concept of a planned socialist economy, wherein the pivotal step was the socialisation of large-scale industries and financial institutions. Coupled with this, he envisioned the rationalisation of production techniques, reminiscent of the Fordist model, which would engender a highly efficient socialist planned economy. Otto Bauer held unwavering confidence in the supremacy of this socialist economic framework over its capitalist counterpart:

So, socialism would firstly change the distribution of the stock of goods as a whole. But this will only be beneficial to the working masses if the production of goods is not hampered simultaneously. Because if we live no better, probably even worse, in a socialist society than under the rule of capital: the fairest distribution could not be of any use to us if there were less to distribute. This means that socialism has its task: it must arrange the distribution of goods more justly, without the production of goods suffering in the process.[1]

Socialisation was not only planned in Austria, but also in Germany. In his inauguration speech as a minister on 19 March 1919, Schumpeter stated that socialisation was now the will of the people and that the overwhelming majority wanted it. He promised the support of the Ministry of Finance to this endeavour and hoped for good cooperation with the head of the socialisation committee, Otto Bauer. He genuinely respected Otto Bauer and held him in high regard as an economist. This professional respect was mutual. An entry in the private diary of Friedrich von Wieser testifies to that:

He [Schumpeter] speaks openly about the cabinet in which he sits. The only intellectual capacity is Otto Bauer, who also respects him back. (You can clearly hear from his words that despite all the contradictions in their opinions, they still value each other as personalities, while they don't respect those around them.) Of Renner, he says that he 'crouches' when Otto Bauer does just raise his voice to speak.[2]

Schumpeter even became a member of the German Socialisation Commission. However, he was, above all, a pragmatist who supported the socialist economic program of the SDAP as a minor evil to a communist revolution, which seemed to be very real in light of the October Revolution in 1917 and the Hungarian and Bavarian ones that reached for Vienna and occurred in the same month as Schumpeter held his speech. Schumpeter expectedly revoked his support for socialisation after this imminent Communist danger was banned from Austria six months later.

The one thing Schumpeter honestly agreed with Otto Bauer on was a property levy (*Vermögensabgabe*). Besides a ruined economy, infrastructure, agri-

1 O. Bauer 1919, p. 3.
2 Schumpeter 1992, p. 7.

cultural production and the colossal burden of war debts tethered to war bonds held by nearly every Austrian citizen, Entente powers expropriated all Austrian assets from the newly established states of the former Empire. Simultaneously, they imposed the unyielding stipulation that Austria shoulder the entire foreign debt bequeathed by the former Empire. This entailed not only payment in foreign currency, an asset in scant supply in Austria, but also at a disadvantageous exchange rate.

Economists across political divisions unanimously held that this set of circumstances amounted to nothing less than the economic annihilation of the fledgling nation. It set a troubling precedent within international credit regulations, notably by assigning the risk of currency depreciation to the creditor rather than the debtor, a deviation deemed unjustified.

Amidst the intricate challenges of the post-war period, another thorny issue surfaced: the matter of servicing the internal war debt. During the war, the Austrian Empire had issued war bonds, which found buyers in a broad spectrum of society, including banks, insurance companies, pension funds, industrialists, small entrepreneurs, and farmers. These investments were motivated by both patriotic fervour and the prospect of substantial returns. Following the dissolution of the Empire, the bondholders retained these securities, facing the looming threat that they might depreciate in value should the new government invalidate them or cease interest payments. Many contended that it was audacious to expect the fledgling state to honour the old war bonds, given the temerity of seeking profit from a lost Imperial war. Helene Bauer counted herself among those who held this perspective. 'The criminal recklessness of yesterday's rulers and their acolytes promised private individuals' interest in the war loan, which in turn gave them an allocation on a portion of the national economy's annual product, which has now reached a staggering height. Even today, despite the loss of power of the previous commanders, and regrettably also the breakdown of the productive forces of the society, it is expected that this recklessness will be rewarded'.[3]

The state default would have been one way out of most of these problems. It would have wiped out all the state's credit obligations. Still, it would have also meant a default of all institutional holders of the war bonds (all banks, credit and insurance institutions, retirement funds etc.), which was a big concern of both Christian Socials and SDAP. Moreover, it would have resulted in bankruptcy for many citizens, particularly those in the petite bourgeoisie and rural households, who had invested in war bonds. In the absence of a

3 Bauer 1919 B, p. 291.

state default, hyperinflation would have led to a similar outcome if no action were taken. Consequently, the property levy emerged as the seemingly sole method to avert state bankruptcy. This levy was intended to apply to assets, with rates ranging between 10 and 80 percent relative to an individual's property. Joseph Schumpeter and Otto Bauer found common ground on this aspect. Nevertheless, there was a profound divergence of opinions regarding the allocation of the funds garnered through the property levy. Helene Bauer proposed a solution whereby holders of war bonds could use them to pay the property tax. This approach would have enabled those holding smaller portions of war bonds to sell them to individuals willing to purchase them for settling their property tax liabilities, thereby mitigating the broader losses that would have befallen these bondholders if the war bonds were eventually invalidated.[4]

As expected, Schumpeter advocated for the use of the funds collected through the property levy to acquire much-needed foreign currency. This foreign currency would serve the dual purpose of stabilising the newly established Austrian currency, the Krone, and reestablishing trust in the financial markets. Additionally, Schumpeter formulated a comprehensive strategy that hinged on the threat of the property levy to compel Austrian financial elites to invest their foreign currency in the Austrian state. He recognised that, given Austria's current credit rating, no financial institution worldwide would extend credit to the newly formed Austrian state. However, he was also aware that private financial elites in Austria still enjoyed a high level of creditworthiness with foreign creditors.

In response to this challenge, Schumpeter introduced a novel state bond that could be purchased using foreign currency and would offset the property levy by offering a stable interest rate. Notably, Otto Bauer was the only economist in the room who immediately grasped the intricacies of Schumpeter's plan. Bauer went even further, suggesting that the interest rate should be set higher than what Schumpeter initially proposed to make the bond more appealing.[5]

In contrast, the Social Democratic Workers' Party (SDAP) advocated for redirecting the funds collected through the property levy towards acquiring large industries from their private owners. This process would serve as remuneration for socialisation, ultimately resulting in the transition of these industries from private ownership to public ownership – a strategy known as socialisation. Under the socialisation plan, the profits generated by these newly social-

4 Bauer 1919 B, p. 292.

5 Schumpeter 1992, p. 322; p. 348.

ised companies would be shared between the employees and the state. One of the key objectives of this approach was to render the existing taxation system obsolete, particularly taxes on 'added value' and other forms of taxation that predominantly burdened the general population through consumption. Instead, the revenue generated by these socialised industries would help support the government and social welfare programs, alleviating the fiscal burden on the masses.

Schumpeter's approach represented a distinctive departure from the prevailing neoclassical economics. To a contemporary reader, it may appear as perfectly rational and logical approach, especially considering the global dominance of neoclassical economics today.

The Austromarxist strategy of socialisation on the other hand may sound strange for a reader raised in post-socialism, but had it been successful, it would have paved the way towards an economy that transcends capitalism. Still it wasn't successful and various factors contributed to that. Before delving into the reasons for the failure of socialisation, it's crucial to examine the significance that this concept held for different Austromarxist economists and the diverse perspectives they had regarding its implementation.

1 Socialisation in Theory

The discourse on socialisation in Germany and Austria proliferated significantly at the end of 1918 and early 1919. In Germany, key figures behind the socialisation strategy included Emil Lederer, Karl Korsch, and the prominent theorist Karl Kautsky. In Austria, Otto Bauer played a pivotal role, along with figures like Otto Leichter, Karl Renner, and numerous others. A diverse group of socialist intellectuals participated in these discussions. However, the ideas of Rudolf Goldscheid had a particularly enduring impact, resonating beyond the socialist sphere.

Rudolf Goldscheid was an independent scholar and the founder of the Viennese Sociological Society, which gathered the most prominent intellectuals of the time, regardless of their political or ideological affiliation. Goldscheid's perspective challenged Marx's view that the primary conflict within capitalism was between capital and labour. Instead, he emphasised the core issue as the conflict between capital and the state. He recognised this from the post-World War I European experience. None of the nations involved in the conflict proved able to effectively tax their wealthy elites to fund the war, which primarily benefited those elites while everyone else suffered. Instead, the costs of the war were shifted onto the working majority through indirect taxes and extensive borrowing from banks owned by the same wealthy elites. These elites continued to profit long after the war ended. Goldscheid's analysis remains highly relevant today. The failure and unwillingness of capitalist democracies to hold those responsible for the 2008 global financial crisis accountable, shifting the burden onto the public, mirrors the inability of the state that Goldscheid discussed in 1925.

> The real social evil lies in the separation of the State from the means of production, in the fact that organized society is barred from ownership of the nation's material wealth. The bourgeois classes have conquered the State by stripping it of its wealth, the working classes must try to conquer it by returning its wealth to it … The decisive revolutionary battle must be fought in the field of the theory and practice of public finance, and in any case, the central doctrines of capitalism are rooted in the science of public finance.[6]

Already in 1917 in his book *State Socialism or State Capitalism*, Goldscheid proposed a highly progressive tax and a property levy (an idea he further developed in 1925) which would amount to between 5 percent and 80 precent of the total property, depending on the size of the property, that would enable the state to purchase a significant proportion of the productive capital and operate it on a profit-making basis. The income would make the state independent of any private financiers and creditors. Indeed, the state would overtake the role of the creditor and would never again need to borrow or issue debt bonds, which would once and for all eliminate its dependence on capital. That part gained Goldscheid the sympathies of none less than Josef Schumpeter (1918) who, while rejecting his idea about state capitalism, nevertheless praised Goldscheid for having established the science of sociology of finances. However, his idea included the provision of a property levy in kind, which would allow the state to nationalise real estate if easier ways were unavailable. This natural levy would transfer one third of the private property over natural resources into the state's hands. This proposal, however, encountered criticism from Helene Bauer. 'The transformation of these donations into money would require an enormous bureaucracy and would cost more than they are worth. In the agricultural case, it would fragment the land into non-contiguous plots, which would make effective cultivation even harder'.[7]

---

6 Goldscheid 1964, p. 291.

7 Bauer 1919 A, p. 271.

Otto Bauer's notion of socialisation was, contrary to Goldscheid, not equal to nationalisation. As per his perspective, the state was the worst manager of the economy one can imagine. The administration of the economy by the state relies on an overly expansive and, consequently, omnipotent bureaucracy, which becomes the instrument for its own ends. The Soviet Union's experiences highlighted the risks associated with this approach.

> Who is to administer the socialised industry? The government? Not at all! If the government controlled all sorts of businesses, it would become too powerful in relation to the people and the people's representatives; such an increase in government power would be dangerous to democracy. And at the same time, the government would mismanage socialised industry; no one manages industrial enterprises worse than the state. That's why we Social Democrats have never called for nationalisation, only socialisation of industry.[8]

Bauer wanted the decision-making to be split up between three interest groups: the employees, the consumers, and the representatives of the state and local government. Experts would lead the technical and financial management of industrial technology. It was essential to socialise the construction land in the cities where the municipal buildings were to be constructed. The previous owners would receive compensation in the form of interest-yielding bonds on the new buildings, which could not be passed on to anyone other than the direct heirs.

While Hilferding advocated starting with the socialisation of banks and financial institutions, Bauer believed that beginning with the socialisation of key industries would be more feasible. He recognised that initiating the socialisation process with financial capital faced significant international constraints. Instead, he proposed starting with industries, which he considered more manageable.

Otto Bauer understood the financial capital concentrated in banks had the power to subdue both governments and big industries to the interests of money capital, and that the socialisation of the banks would channel this power back into society. But he was aware that the new state's vaults were empty and that nobody would credit a bankrupt state with ravaged industry. Hence, the private Austrian banks were the only channel through which foreign credit could have reached Austrian industry. With this in mind, the socialisation of industries was

8 O. Bauer 1919, p. 5.

maybe not a first choice but remained the only realistic one. He envisioned that industries could be socialised first, and once their stability was established, the banks could be socialised without the need for expropriation. This could be achieved by replacing the shareholders in the banks' decision-making bodies with committees comprising representatives from the state, industrial councils, agricultural associations, consumer groups, and workers' and employees' unions.[9]

2 Socialisation in Practice

The property levy and socialisation were announced at the beginning of 1919 in all SDAP close media outlets. This prompted panic among the property elites, who did everything in their power to undermine it. Otto Bauer announced that the first company to be socialised would be Alpine Montane Society (exploitation of iron ore). He chose this company because the withdrawal of its Czech proprietaries placed it entirely in the hands of the Austrian capitalists, which meant less pressure from abroad. Additionally, the worth of its shares was low given the situation of Austrian industry after the war. On the other side, the minister of finances, Joseph Schumpeter, made steps to acquire bitterly needed foreign currency. He secretly appointed private banker Richard Cola and his bank Cola & Co. to buy foreign currencies for 50 million Krone for the Ministry of Finances. Cola purchased on the European shadow markets in Zürich and Amsterdam for better exchange rates and to support the ministry. However, Cola & Co. traded shares in addition to currency. He was a broker for the biggest shareholder of the Alpine Montane Society, the Lower Austrian Eskompte Society.[10]

Cola sold the majority of the Alpine shares to an Italian Group behind the back of the government. As soon as this information became public, it sparked a widespread outcry not only among SDAP (whose plans to socialise the Alpine Montane Society were thwarted), but also among other segments of society (who deemed such a transaction to be a high-level act of treason). In his book The Austrian Revolution, Otto Bauer blamed Schumpeter for having consciously subverted socialisation with this move. The sale of the Alpine Montane Society escalated into an affair that tainted Schumpeter's reputation. The government formed a committee to look into the accusations of treason against Schumpeter, but they ultimately did not confirm Schumpeter's guilt.

9 O. Bauer 1919, p. 24. The same as above – "Der Weg zum Sozialismus".

10 Chaloupek 2016, p. 18.

Alpine was a joint-stock company, not a state-owned entity, which meant that its shares were tradable on the market. The commission concluded that, even if he wanted to, Schumpeter could not have prevented the sale. Additionally, Cola claimed he did not know he was selling the shares to Italians. However, his actions not only delivered a company of strategic interest for the state into the hands of the Italians, who were still enemies at this point, but also raised the value of remaining shares so that the remuneration of the private shareholders became de facto impossible.

After this significant setback put an end to the socialisation plans in the big industries, not much more remained to be socialised. Some companies were transferred to the status of public companies, like 'Österreichische Werke' and 'Fischameder Werke', which produced construction materials for housing projects. Karl Renner, in his speech on 19 October 1919, pointed out that the majority of the wealth owned by the rich consisted of paper assets, particularly war bonds. He emphasised that these assets were, in reality, liabilities rather than true assets. This realisation led Renner to conclude that it was impossible to socialise the debts. This was the end of the socialisation plan. 17 October 1919 – the day of the ratification of the (for Austria) devastating Saint Germain peace accord – saw the resignation of both the Austrian government and the Socialisation Commission.

The failure of socialisation prompted numerous Austromarxists to investigate the underlying causes. The one by Käthe Leichter stood out, as she didn't just try to figure out what went wrong but also drew on the lessons learned from running public companies like 'Österreichische Werke' in Vienna, which were managed according to Otto Bauer's plan, one third by the workers, one third by the consumer associations, and one third by the state. According to Leichter (1927), despite the fact that socialisation was not carried out as planned or hoped for on a national scale, the public-run companies such as 'Österreichische Werke', 'Fischamender Werke', or GESIBA were instrumental in facilitating significant housing projects for the Municipality of Vienna under the governance of SDAP. These projects became emblematic of the accomplishments of the 'Red Vienna' and continue to be one of its most prominent symbols.

Karl Renner, during 1919, was deeply involved in the Saint-Germain peace negotiations, serving as the Prime Minister and leading the Austrian delegation. Therefore, he didn't actively participate in the socialisation debate at that time. However, he later published an extensive socialisation theory in 1924, following the failure of Otto Bauer's socialisation project. Having learned from the experiences of both the Austrian and German socialisation initiatives, Renner came to the conclusion that socialisation should not commence with large industries or banks alone. Instead, it needed to encompass the entire process of economic circulation. The capitalist system, according to Marx, had a closed circuit of circulation of capital, which consisted of several steps, including planning, financing, production, and distribution. According to Renner, the Austrian socialisation plan failed because it was too specific and concentrated on the production side of the economy, thereby neglecting the distribution side, i.e., the totality of the circulation process.

It is evident that the process of circulation is the ultimate legislator and judge of capitalist society, and it is the genuine issue of socialisation. *It realises the value and added value; it distributes these to the economic agents; it is the final authority on the economic destiny of everyone*! The socialisation that does not start from it misses the supreme purpose and must therefore miss it. If we were to socialise the production plants and maintain the circulation process as it is, the anarchic market and the law of value and surplus value that anonymously governs it would remain our judge thereafter.[11]

Renner's insights on socialisation in 1927 foreshadowed issues that would prove critical for socialist systems in post-World War II Europe. In these systems, socialised and nationalised enterprises under workers' control encountered challenges related to distributing their products in the anarchic world markets. Renner also delved into a fundamental feature of the capitalist system: the concept of added value. He recognised that added value was at the heart of the capitalist mode of production, driving the constant need for more production to sustain itself. Renner grappled with the question of how to create a new system that would break free from this perpetual expansion and waste, inherent to capitalism, and instead produce only what society genuinely needed. This question has become even more pertinent in our contemporary era than it was in the early twentieth century.

Helene Bauer went even further in this regard. She realised that a socialist system is not feasible in a single country, especially if it's small and dependent on global financial and trade networks. 'Moreover, the events in Russia and Hungary raise the question anew as to whether socialism can be realised in any other way than on an international basis'.[12] The power of international capital and its ability to impose regulations on international retail chains that Bauer recognised mirrors the influence it wields in today's world through institutions like the World Trade Organization and various international agreements. Moreover, she acknowledged its capacity to support reactionary forces in both capitalist and socialist countries, which is evident from numerous historical

11 Renner 1924, pp. 338–9. I made a mistake it is 1924 – already listed in the bibliography.

12 Bauer 1919 C, p. 342.

examples of U.S. involvement in regime changes in Latin America during the twentieth century, including Chile, Nicaragua, and El Salvador, among others. Helene Bauer's assertion that the power of international finance is a formidable element within this arsenal of influence that renders individual countries relatively powerless has been borne out by history and remains a salient observation.

'The bourgeois democrats of the West possess a profound comprehension of the international conditionality of the interests of capital and this is why socialism, even in countries where the proletariat appears to have completely overcome the resistance of its own bourgeoisie, is not solely a matter of organisation, but remains a matter of power ... And it is not about the confession of the starving masses to the 'nutritional obligation' (Josef Popper – Lynkeus), to the 'levy in kind' (Rudolf Goldscheid) or to the 'Central Economic Office' (Otto Neurath), but rather the question of when the International of Labour as an effective force will be able to oppose the International of Capital, which is already in action.'[13]

---

13 Bauer 1919 C, p. 3. The names enclosed within parentheses are the authors notes and refer to the authors who advocated for these concepts.

CHAPTER 5

Otto Neurath and Money Economy

Otto Neurath was equally comfortable in both the Austromarxist Circle and the Vienna Circle. He made significant contributions to pictography in statistics, political economy, and social research. In 1922 Neurath published an article on the money economy in socialism in the journal *Der Kampf* titled 'Money and Socialism' (orig. *Geld und Sozialismus*). In the same year, Helene Bauer published a reply to his treatise in the same journal. Her basic line of argument was, again, primarily methodological. She contended that Neurath had misconstrued the crux of Marx's methodology, encapsulated in the concept of dialectical materialism, resulting in erroneous conclusions concerning Marx's vision of a monetary economy within a socialist framework. She also accused him of a flawed understanding of socialism as an interim stage between capitalism and the emerging social order forged through conflict. She maintained that the concept of socialism should not be prematurely concretized but rather allowed to take shape through future struggles, resisting any attempts to predetermine it. In Helene Bauer's perspective, Marx's inquiries were primarily directed toward discerning the conditions necessary to transcend bourgeois society, as opposed to outlining the prerequisites of a future classless state. "The working class has no ideals to realize; it only has to set free the elements of the new society that have already developed in the womb of the collapsing bourgeoisie class."[1] It is noteworthy to mention that Otto Neurath initiated a debate on socialist economy that went beyond the circles of socialist economists. Mises famous text on the socialist economy, 'Economic Calculation in Socialist Community,' from 1920, was an attempt to prove the socialist economy unviable. It was a part of the debate that unfolded in the Journal Archive.

Helene Bauer maintained the conviction that Marx conveyed the notion that the working class could achieve its emancipation and elevated states of existence exclusively through sustained and resolute endeavors. This endeavor involved a sequence of revolutionary processes, culminating in the comprehensive alteration of both individuals and their societal conditions. She asserted that Marx was staunchly opposed to the notion of fashioning preconceived utopian visions for future generations and epochs, which would be implemented through popular mandates.

1 Bauer 1922 A, p. 195.

'For all those who wanted to delight people with their self-made concepts for fighting capitalism and making a more purposeful society, he had nothing but ridicule and scorn; for, according to Marx, the liberation of the working class must be the work of the working class and the new society must arise in the struggle. The sparse remarks in his works on the nature of a socialist economic order have no socio-technical but purely conceptual character; they are not building blocks but antitheses'.[2]

These passages underscore another pivotal point in Helene Bauer's vision of socialism. Central to her perspective was an unwavering resistance to the notion of the new social order being instituted through majority rule or under the directive of a political party, mirroring the Soviet Union's approach. She vehemently contested the idea that the political majority should wield the authority to prescribe or enforce an economic framework. Rather, she advocated for such a system to organically emerge from the trials and tribulations of the proletariat, emphasizing that it should not even be meticulously devised before these struggles, let alone imposed through a decree. This stance showcased her profound aversion to teleological thinking and a rejection of any form of determinism concerning the outcomes of future struggles. Most notably, she stood firmly against the imposition of any preconceived economic model of the present onto the unfolding struggles of the future. In her view, forthcoming developments would give rise to novel models that could not be preconceived or formulated prior to these transformative events.

It is noteworthy that Otto Neurath shared a similar anti-teleological perspective in his general theory of social systems. In his overarching worldview, particularly reflected in his ethical stance, Neurath aligned himself with Epicureanism. The Austromarxists exhibited a wide spectrum of epistemological approaches, ranging from Max Adler's Neokantianism to a more open dialectical materialism closely akin to Ernst Mach rather than Lenin, as advocated by Karl Kautsky. Others adhered to Scientific Positivism combined with Critical Rationalism, such as Friedrich Adler and Gustav Eckstein, Edgar Zeisel, and also Otto Neurath, while Otto Bauer espoused a materialist syncretism.

In his 1928 book titled 'Lifestyle and Class Struggle' (orig. title 'Lebensgestaltung und Klassenkampf'), one chapter was dedicated to exploring the relationship between Karl Marx and Epicurus. Since Marx had written his dissertation on Epicurus, a connection between the two philosophers naturally presented itself. Nevertheless, it was Otto Neurath who became the first Marxist thinker to definitively establish this connection. He posited that Marx was not a determin-

2 Ibid.

ist, as many assumed due to his Hegelian influences, but rather a proponent of philosophical openness. Neurath rejected the idea that Marx was a philosopher of social apriorism, as proposed by Max Adler, who believed that the social character of individuals was inherently predetermined and could be realized through proper education. Instead, Neurath contended that while social inclusion could lead to human happiness, it could also burden individuals with connections they might seek to discard.[3] Otto Neurath perceived Marxism through the lens of Social Epicureanism, conceiving it as an art aimed at securing happiness for both individual human beings and humanity as a whole. He contended that this pursuit of happiness was hindered by the capitalist system of exploitation. During his time, Neurath stood as the singular Marxist philosopher who steered Marxism toward an Epicurean direction. It wasn't until the early 1980s that Louis Althusser forged a comparable linkage, identifying a radical anti-teleological approach he termed 'aleatoric materialism' in the early works of Marx.[4]

His Epicurean inclinations are discernible in his economic theory, notably in the juxtaposition of a capitalist system reliant on pure profit accounting and a socialist model emphasizing utility or usefulness accounting. In the socialist paradigm, utility estimations are derived from assessments of the economy as a whole, with a primary focus on the quality of life that society aspires to provide for all its members. Consequently, it becomes imperative to meticulously define the societal standard of living to accurately gauge the utility of an economy. This precision stands in stark contrast to capitalism, notorious for its often chaotic production practices, frequently resulting in goods being discarded directly into the waste stream.

His economic theory was influenced by the social reformer Carl Ballod and according to the historian Ernst Glaser to some extent, especially in the disinclination for money by his father, economist Wilhelm Neurath.[5] Furthermore, Otto Neurath's reflections on the wartime economy, a subject of his study during World War I, played a significant role in the development of his concept of 'War Socialism'. Notably, this notion drew criticism not only from Helene Bauer but also from various other Austromarxists, including Otto and Käthe Leichter and Karl Kautsky. Neurath's perspective diverged from the 1919 Social Democratic Workers' Party (SDAP) vision, which focused on the socialization of major industries. In contrast, Neurath argued that comprehensive socialization

3 Neurath 1928, p. 41.

4 Althusser 1996; Larise 2007.

5 Glaser 1981, p. 224.

should encompass all industries across the nation, leading to the establishment of a moneyless economy. To achieve this, he believed it was imperative to formulate an all-encompassing economic framework and institute a 'Central Economic Agency' (Zentralwirtschaftsamt), capable of replacing the monetary system with a system based on 'universal statistics'.

Critics, such as Karl Kautsky and Otto Leichter, decried Neurath's plan as resembling a form of military regimentation. Helene Bauer, on the other hand, presented a distinct line of critique. She contended that monetary reform alone would not bring about significant change. Such reforms, she argued, would fail to address the fundamental issue of capitalist exploitation because capitalism and its monetary system were deeply intertwined. Consequently, she asserted that it was impossible to successfully alter the monetary system without first overcoming capitalism itself, a stance she derived from the teachings of Marx and Engels.

'Marx and Engels ruthlessly criticized all attempts to eradicate the damages of capitalism through mere monetary reform. On the contrary, they showed how, given the intrinsic ties between capitalist commodity production and the capitalist monetary system, the monetary reform alone could not amend the damage without eradicating the capitalist system of production in the process as well. Thus, they saw the socialist monetary reform merely as an attempt to dissolve socialism into a fundamental misunderstanding between merchandise and money (footnote: Marx, On the Critique of Political Economy, page 73).'[6]

Helene Bauer, in her quest for conceptual clarity, found Marx's "Anti-Dühring" to offer a preliminary outline for the eventual overthrow of capitalism. However, she emphasized that in the transition period, before capitalism had been fully dismantled, another facet of Marx's work became paramount. This aspect was notably highlighted in Marx's concise polemical work, 'On the German Workers' Party'. Otto Neurath also made reference to this text in his article, but H. Bauer contended that he drew an opposing interpretation from Marx himself. In this work, Marx delineated a boundary between the dialectical method for comprehending history and the French utopianism epitomized by Ferdinand Lassalle. Marx maintained that safeguarding production necessitated an alignment of the producers' entitlement to the communal product with the same metric as the labor contributed, despite the inherent disparities among individuals. This is precisely why, according to Helene Bauer, money remained a prerequisite in socialism, serving as a tool for the rational planning of the socialized economy.

6 Bauer 1922 A, p. 127.

As the role of property evolved, it was expected that the social functions of all institutions built upon the foundation of private property would likewise undergo a transformation within a new socialist society. In this reimagined socialist framework, the monetary system, once used by capitalists to procure labor and accumulate profits, would be repurposed to facilitate a rational work plan and equitable distribution. And further: 'The distribution (of working hours) is based on an arithmetic calculation, which is only possible if the entire production process has also been carried out arithmetically, that means if it is based on a monetary order'.[7]

One of the primary shortcomings in Otto Neurath's vision of a moneyless economy was his near-exclusive focus on money's function as a medium of exchange, a role he considered obsolete in a socialist context. In contrast, Helene Bauer underscored the significance of money as the unit of account. She saw Neurath as a scholar whose aversion to money extended to the point where he was willing to banish it from the world, even if this entailed forsaking arithmetic altogether. From her perspective, Neurath's economic blueprint aimed to transcend the prevailing capitalist-bourgeois ideology by mandating the abandonment of every unit of account.

'So Neurath throws swamps, streets, animals, and people into one pot. While the evil capitalist, who pays for everything with money, finds a mathematical expression for everything, the socialist can only record this pulp and what comes out of it statistically. He does not differentiate between people, tools, natural working conditions, things, and humans are to him as indiscriminately present as they are present to the capitalist who buys them or the warlord who commands them: five horses, ten men!'[8]

Undiscriminating and undifferentiated calculation not only presents mathematical impracticality and potential risks for a planned economy but, as per H. Bauer's perspective, it also paves the way for authoritarianism. In a system devoid of a unit of account and the necessary differentiation in production elements, there is a looming likelihood that a central commanding authority becomes indispensable for economic calculation. This, in turn, sets the stage for the emergence of authoritarianism within the economic framework.

Helene Bauer did not cling to the notion of money as it existed in capitalist and earlier societal models. Instead, she had a visionary perspective that transcended her era, envisioning a form of money that would not be tethered to any material commodity and perhaps not even to a specific state, as a likely out-

7 Bauer 1922 A, p. 199.
8 Bauer 1922 A, p. 200.

come of future developments. Nonetheless, she remained a pragmatic thinker in the Machiavellian tradition, prioritizing the consideration of imminent challenges of her time over speculating about possibilities that may or may not materialize in a distant future.

In her response to Otto Neurath, she concluded by raising a far more urgent and prescient issue. She contemplated how socialist nations could adapt to survive and thrive in a world overwhelmingly dominated by the capitalist economy, positioning themselves as socialist entities within a vast sea of capitalism. Her foresight underscored the challenges socialist nations would face in navigating the complex landscape of a capitalist world in the cold war era. 'The transition from the capitalist to the socialist world economy is not an immediate possibility for us to consider, but the conditions of existence of proletarian states amid a bourgeois environment ...'[9] Indeed, Helene Bauer's foresight appears almost prophetic, for not only did she anticipate the evolution of fiat money and cryptocurrencies, but she also highlighted an issue that would eventually contribute to the downfall of socialist economies in the 1990s. This issue revolved around the fundamental incompatibility of isolated socialist economies with the progressively globalized capitalist system of economic and financial regulations that began to take shape in the 1980s. These very same challenges continue to be pertinent and pressing for the socialist Left well into the twenty-first century.

9 Bauer 1922 A, p. 201.

CHAPTER 6

Imperialism

After the first wave of imperialism debates which preceded World War I, imperialism once again became a central theme in Marxist thought from the mid-1920s to the early 1930s, The imperialism debates of the first (and partly even the second) wave were often closely linked to the context of colonialism and often used the terms interchangeably. In 1913, Rosa Luxemburg's book *The Accumulation of Capital: A Contribution to the Economic Explanation of Imperialism* was published, significantly shaping the Marxist discourse on imperialism in the years leading up to World War I. Luxemburg's argument posited that, due to the weak purchasing power of the working population, developed capitalist countries could produce more than they could sell in their own markets. This concept, known as the under-consumption paradigm, has its roots in the ideas of the nineteenth-century Swiss economist Simone de Sismondi, who also predicted that new markets in pre-capitalist countries would eventually become saturated, leading to a halt in expansion and a crisis of overproduction. Similar notions can be traced throughout the nineteenth century, with figures such as activist Louis Blanc in 1848, Auguste Blanqui in the 1880s, Moses Hess, Thomas Robert Malthus, and the social reformer Carl Rodbertus (who directly established the cause-and-effect relationship between under-consumption and imperialism). According to Schröder, Rodbertus was a favourite economist of the young Rosa Luxemburg.[1] Malthus and Rodbertus introduced the idea that capitalism requires 'third persons' that consume their products but do not derive their livelihood from capitalist production. Rosa Luxemburg incorporated this concept into her own analysis of capitalism. This idea underscores the necessity for external consumers, beyond the immediate circle of production, to absorb the surplus output of the capitalist system.

Marx and Engels incorporated the under-consumption theory into their theory of capitalist accumulation. In this theory, capitalists use their profits, or in Marx's terms, surplus value, for two main purposes: first, for personal consumption and, second, for further investment in the production apparatus. The latter is what Marx referred to as 'accumulation'. However, as production and the development of productive forces continue to expand, the purchasing power of both workers and capitalists increases at a slower rate than production output. This leads to a situation where the market becomes saturated with goods for

1 Schröder 1973, p. 14.

which there is insufficient demand. Profit margins begin to decline and an economic crisis unfolds. Marx underscored the significance of under-consumption in his theory of cyclical crises within the capitalist system. He formulated a schema of accumulation in the Second Volume of *Capital*. Unfortunately, this schema, like many other works by Marx, remained incomplete and became a bone of contention among subsequent Marxist theorists.

Rosa Luxemburg adopted Marx's schema, which posited that overproduction would lead to reduced investments, subsequently causing a continuous decline in profits and leading to economic crises. From this, she deduced that the collapse of capitalism would be inevitable unless new markets for goods were discovered. This is because, in her analysis, production continues to increase while markets remain limited. Consequently, capital is driven to seek markets in previously non-capitalist countries to avert its own collapse. Luxemburg's thesis, later revisited and expanded upon by scholars like Fritz Sternberg and Henryk Grossman in Austria after World War I, highlighted that the ultimate collapse of capitalism was a result of the imbalance between supply and demand. Even when new markets in previously non-capitalist countries were accessed, these markets would eventually become saturated, exacerbating the crisis.

Rudolf Hilferding, who authored *Finance Capital* in 1910, introduced a new chapter in Marxist political economy. He rejected the notion of an inevitable collapse of the capitalist system, emphasising the increasing financialisation of the economy, which would fundamentally alter how capitalism functions. In his work, Hilferding pointed to the growing role of finance in the capitalist economy. Karl Kautsky, who complemented Hilferding's ideas, envisioned the development of international cartels and trusts within the organisation of capital. These international entities would dominate and monopolise national markets, leading to the concept of global 'Ultra-Imperialism'. This idea was influenced by the theory of imperialism formulated by John A. Hobson, a liberal political economist whose work also had a significant impact on Lenin's theory of imperialism. Another economist influenced by Hobson's ideas on imperialism was Josef Schumpeter, who belonged to the liberal spectrum. Helene Bauer's theories of imperialism can be situated within this perspective, contrasting with those developed by Rosa Luxemburg. Rather than predicting capitalism's inevitable collapse, this perspective emphasises its transformation through financialisation and the development of supranational economic entities.[2]

2 For a more thorough account of theories of imperialism in Austromarxism see my article in forthcoming special edition of Historical Materialism Journal on Austromarxism.

Helene Bauer authored four texts on imperialism: 'Imperialist War' (1924), 'Imperialism' (1927), 'Accumulation, Credit, and Imperialism' (1927), and 'International Capital Concentration and the Leninist Theory of Imperialism as Catastrophe' (1930). Among these texts, the 1929 addition, 'Another theoretician of collapse', discusses Henryk Grossman, who revived Rosa Luxemburg's theory of a necessary collapse of capitalism due to insufficient consumption (under-consumption). This theory also suggests that imperialism is necessary for the survival of capitalism. Bauer's texts challenge two of Rosa Luxemburg's key theses: the idea that capitalism will collapse due to its internal contradictions and the necessity of imperialism to address the crisis of accumulation. Two other texts from 1924 and 1928 focus on the theory of imperialist war and present a counterargument to Lenin's theories, which propose that war is a necessary consequence of imperialism. In her 1924 text, Helene Bauer lays the foundations for her own theory of imperialism, which she further develops in subsequent texts. Helene Bauer was skeptical of Rosa Luxemburg's conception of imperialism in capitalism, suspecting that it was based on false assumptions made by capitalists themselves. While Luxemburg's theory suggested that colonies were important markets for their goods, Bauer argued the opposite, that is, that the markets provided by colonies were actually negligible in size. Therefore, she believed that Luxemburg's theory was constructed on completely erroneous foundations. Bauer writes:

> The political possession of a colony may indeed be decisive in granting concessions of all kinds, and thereby certainly benefits specific groups of capitalists. However, it does not guarantee the motherland's industry the sale of its goods and the supply of raw materials, nor does it ensure a lasting advantage in trade ... Despite the fierce competition posed by foreign industries, especially the export onslaught of continental cartels on English capital, access to English markets and protectorates following the motherland's trade policy remained open. Envy and animosity did not culminate in the abandonment of the 'open door' policy, although it would have been the easiest means of defence.[3]
>
> Thus, one's own colonial territory increasingly becomes an area for all.[4]

Her assessment is based on the trade balances of the pre-war years, which clearly show that domestic trade, as well as trade with equally developed and

3 Bauer 1924 A pp. 386–7.

4 Bauer 1924 A, p. 387.

independent countries, far exceeded trade with colonial territories. It is also evident that colonial powers imported much more from their colonial territories than they exported to them.

The colonial territories of the European Great Powers, acquired during the era of 'modern imperialism', occupied such a small space in the foreign trade of their motherland that their possession could not contribute to industrial development or provide a secure outlet for capital exports. The major items in exports to the colonies were limited to British India, Canada, and Australia, all countries that had been conquered by Europeans in the era of primitive plunder without the aid of modern banking mechanisms. Today, with the exception of British India, they are no longer colonies in reality but have become independent states with their own administration. In Germany's export of goods, which amounted to approximately 10 billion Marks in 1913, we see the African protectorates, which occupied such a significant place in the imagination of colonial politicians, represented by the modest figure of only 144 million Marks. Meanwhile, small but highly industrialised Belgium was importing goods from Germany worth 500 million Marks.[5]

And further: 'The expansion of English possessions abroad did not occur through capital exports but by deferring foreign interest payments. However, the English market's capacity, in terms of value, significantly exceeded the value of its production: its imports have been greater than its exports for decades'.[6]

Helene Bauer aimed to empirically refute the assertion of the necessity of imperialism for capitalism's survival and to demonstrate the harmful effects of this assumption. If one assumes that colonisation primarily serves to create new markets, thus ensuring an increasing production capacity in the colonial motherlands, then an imperial war would appear rational from an economic perspective. Helene Bauer reminds her reader that this was precisely the argument put forth by the warmongering parties before World War I. The German Empire used this claim to present the population with a false choice: colonisation or stagnation. However, the facts were quite different: 'Measured against the vast scale of commodity and capital turnover within European countries, within Europe and America before the outbreak of war, all colonial acquisitions, all the contentious objects of world politics, economically played a ridiculously insignificant role'.[7]

A segment of the working class embraced the idea of supporting colonial expansion because it held the promise of improving the living standards of

5 Bauer 1924 A, p. 386.
6 Bauer 1924 A, p. 387.
7 Bauer 1924 A, p. 388.

workers in the colonial motherlands. This perspective came to be known as 'social imperialism'. Meanwhile, another part of the working class supported imperialism because they believed that capitalism would eventually reach the limits of its expansion, as predicted by Rosa Luxemburg, and saw imperialism as a path to imminent collapse. The imperial war for colonies was widely believed to be driven by economic necessity. However, the economic reality was quite different. In the context of modern production conditions and global trade networks, the economy was no longer a fierce competition of all against all but rather an intricate interweaving of international production and trade chains: 'The 'envy of trade' as a political motive may have played a role in antiquity, where the complete eradication of the defeated enemy after a victorious war was also part of state policy. However, in the dealings of modern states with each other, forced by the international interweaving of economies to rehabilitate the defeated enemy to avoid losing buyers and sellers, it belongs only in the textbook for loyal patriots, and the same textbook is served to us by the communist theory too'.[8] In regarding the competition between the capitalist states as detrimental for capital as a world system, Helene Bauer follows line of argumentation similar to Karl Kautsky, who states that '... the capitalist economy is seriously threatened precisely by the contradictions between its States. Every far-sighted capitalist today must call on his fellows: capitalists of all countries, unite!'[9]

Helene Bauer proposed a socio-economic explanatory model that diverged from the rational, economic explanation of the causes of World War I. She argued that economic factors were not the primary drivers of the war. Instead, it was the feudal ambitions of aristocratic and military elites that prevailed, even in the face of economic rationality. The irrational, old-imperial, romanticised concept of martial heroism coupled with the financial interests of the military-industrial complex seeking quick profits were the true driving forces behind World War I. 'The war industry serves the need for war, just as alcohol capital serves alcoholism'.[10] So, the main cause of World War I was not economic necessity, but rather the opposite—the dominance of politics over economics. As Bauer writes, '... that eventually the world war, for which there was no immediate cause, could ignite due to the arms race and mobilisation, now points to the significant separation of the economy from politics and the prevailing position of politics over the economy in the countries whose governments bear responsibility and complicity for the global conflagration'.[11]

8 Bauer 1928, p. 397.
9 Kautsky 1914, p. 920.
10 Bauer 1924 A, p. 389.
11 Bauer 1924 A, p. 388.

Helene Bauer argued that during World War I, the interests of certain capitalist classes in securing access to raw materials through military confrontation ran contrary to the interests of capitalism as a system based on the world market and a rule-based trading order. She believed that the imperialist war industry had displaced the capitalist peace industry, which was also an economic reality. In contrast to thinkers like Rosa Luxemburg and Lenin, who believed that capitalism had an inherent tendency toward war, Helene Bauer, much like Joseph Schumpeter (1919), assumed that capitalism was neither necessarily nor inherently belligerent. 'Capitalism, in alliance with feudal powers, can be bellicose, aiming to increase its profit rate through war and actively seeking war. However, it can also be peaceful, aiming to gain new markets with state credit guarantees for dealings with countries whose legal status raises suspicions, all without military backing, or it can strive for profits through international cartels, quota allocation, and profit protection'.[12]

Helene Bauer strongly disagreed with Lenin's idea of 'social imperialism' and argued against it. She attempted to demonstrate, using the example of England, that colonial rule did not necessarily lead to an improvement in the living standards of the working class in the colonial motherland. She accused Lenin of failing to distinguish between the interests of the ruling class and those of the entire nation. She argued that capitalists often presented their own interests as the national interest. In her view, Lenin had fallen for this deception by not making this crucial distinction.

The capitalist rentier class can invest income from foreign holdings domestically, but it can also, as the American example shows, squander it abroad. Instead of hiring new workers in their own country, they can exploit foreigners and use their cheaper labour to render their own workforce unemployed. However, they lie everywhere, transforming their own profit interest into an economic interest of their country, from which they demand protection of their property, all in line with Lenin's doctrine.[13]

Helene Bauer's theory of imperialism, influenced by Rudolf Hilferding's ideas, went beyond the traditional understanding of imperialism as simply colonialism. She recognised finance capital as a driving force behind a new imperialism, one that preferred politically independent states over traditional colonies. These independent states were integrated into the financial networks and cartels of finance capitalism, creating a context of financial dependence. In this form of imperialism, the emphasis was not on industrial goods but on fin-

12 Bauer 1927 A, p. 12.

13 Bauer 1928, p. 399.

ancial products, especially credit. Helene Bauer anticipated the central role of credit in this post-colonial imperialism, which would replace traditional colonial imperialism and become the dominant form of imperialism in the second half of the twentieth century and beyond.

Helene Bauer's recognition of the central role of credit in the new imperialism marked a departure from earlier theories that focused on classical exchange relationships and the imbalance between commodity production and consumption. Even two decades after Rosa Luxemburg's book on the subject, some theorists like Fritz Sternberg still believed they could derive the collapse of capitalism from these traditional factors. However, Helene Bauer's perspective highlighted the evolving dynamics of capitalism, where finance and credit played a more significant role in shaping economic relationships and imperialism. 'The credit that modern credit banks provide to industry, i.e., operating and investment credit, is, if we disregard the actual savings deposits, which play no significant role, a creation of purchasing power'.[14] Furthermore: 'Anyone who, like Sternberg, assumes that a commodity is unsellable because they cannot spot an exchangeable counterpart in their vicinity confuses, in their thinking, the modern circulation process, which is only a lever of production and distribution, with the exchange of primitives!'[15]

Helene Bauer's observation of capital internationalisation is a crucial insight into the changing dynamics of the global economy after World War I. The financial support provided to defeated powers by the victorious ones as a means to secure their own economies reflects the complex and interconnected nature of modern capitalism. This financial support was not merely about trade or foreign investments but demonstrated how the financial system and credit relationships played a central role in shaping the post-war economic landscape. It also highlights the interdependence and shared interests among different nations and how they used financial mechanisms to maintain stability and avoid economic collapse. 'This gave rise to the international financing of various national industries by a diverse pool of capital that aimed not to promote and favour specific state-defined economic interests but to secure the internationally raised loan capital and its dividends. The same role that national financial groups played in national cartels must now fall to the new international financial groups on an international scale'.[16] The emergence of various international cartels and syndicates like European railroad cartel, copper syndicates,

14 Bauer 1927 B, p. 176.
15 Ibid.
16 Bauer 1928, p. 393.

and others, is a testament to the growing economic interdependence and globalisation during the early twentieth century. These cartels and syndicates represented collaborative arrangements between businesses and industries across national borders. They were often established to regulate production, prices, and market shares in order to maximise profits and avoid destructive competition.

Amid World War I, the international steel consortium, comprising the majority of European steel manufacturers, delivered steel to multiple battlefronts. Helene Bauer perceived these instances as indicative of an emerging phase of capital internationalisation that attained heightened prominence during the 1920s. This perspective diverged from subsequent classical realist paradigms in international politics, as well as Lenin's conventional Marxist framework, which predominantly construed capitalist imperialism as a contest among national factions of capitalist elites. Instead, Bauer's analysis underscored the ascendance of transnational economic dynamics and their cooperative influence in shaping the global economic landscape during this era.

'The financing of industry by internationally mixed capital is increasingly seen as more than just a by-product of financial operations carried out by a bank or a specific national financial group to attract foreign funds for their own purposes. International financial trusts (investment trusts), in which banks from multiple countries pool a portion of their capital for international ventures and create a common international organisation, represent the new form of capital export, the new means of conquering markets, and, in short, capital expansion that escapes the influence of competition'.[17] Furthermore: 'In the phase of high capitalism, the concentration of capital breaks through the geopolitically often senseless borders of states, becoming a high concentration that completes capitalism's historical task, the establishment of the world market'.[18]

17 Bauer 1928, p. 394.
18 Ibid.

CHAPTER 7

Crisis in World Economy

1 On the Crisis in World Economy and Fascism

The unprecedented economic crisis that ensued in the wake of the New York Stock Exchange crash in 1929 paved the way for the emergence of various crisis theories from virtually every school of economic thought. Within this landscape, neoclassical theorists aimed to assign blame to the state's profligacy and overly generous social benefits for the economic quagmire. Meanwhile, socialist economists delved into the causes of the crisis, attributing it to factors such as financial speculation, the inherent propensity of the capitalist mode of production to cyclical crises, and the chaotic irrationality of the capitalist market economy.

In 1931, the initial segment of his crisis analysis was presented by Otto Bauer in a work titled *Rationalisation and Failed Rationalisation* (*Rationalisierung und Fehlrationalisierung*). His primary contention revolved around the capitalist economy's inability to rationalise the market economy due to an unceasing pursuit of maximum profit, thereby subjecting the economy to a state of anarchy where profitability took precedence over genuine social productivity. Bauer's book aimed to provide a preliminary outline, rather than offering an exhaustive examination of all the factors contributing to a crisis. A more comprehensive analysis was intended to follow. However, Austrofascist police confiscated his nearly completed manuscript for the second part of the book in 1934, leading to the belief that it had been destroyed.

In response, he authored another book titled *Between Two Wars?* in which he integrated portions from the lost manuscript based on his memory while in exile in 1936. Unexpectedly, the manuscript was not destroyed, and it found its way through adventurous routes into the possession of the International Institute for Social History in Amsterdam, where it was safeguarded during World War II. Remarkably, it remains unpublished to this day.

The most significant crisis in history prompted some Marxist economists to entertain hopes of an inevitable collapse of capitalism. This anticipation, not new within Marxist theories, rested on the belief that capitalism would prove incapable of enduring a crisis of such magnitude and would ultimately succumb to its inherent contradictions. This notion had its roots in the ideas put forth by Rosa Luxemburg in 1913, who argued that the anarchy inherent in the capitalist system would inevitably lead to its downfall. Henryk Grossman, an economist associated with the broader Austromarxist circle, rekindled the theory of collapse in the late 1920s. He was part of the team at Grünberg's Frankfurt Institute for Social Research. Grossman expounded the thesis of the inevitable collapse of the capitalist system in his 1929 work, *The Law of Accumulation and Collapse of Capitalist System* (*Der Akkumulations- und Zusammenbruchsgesetz des kapitalistischen Systems*), and continued to develop this theory, even after returning from exile in the United States to Leipzig, until his passing in 1949. However, two unorthodox Marxist economists, Helene Bauer and Natalie Moszkowska (a Polish-born economist based in Switzerland who engaged with Austromarxists in 1930 and subsequently contributed to publications like *Kampf* and *Arbeit und Wirtschaft*) emerged as prominent critics of Grossman's theory of collapse.

Helene Bauer vehemently rejected Grossman's theory, primarily due to its implausibility and its incongruence with Marx's own rudimentary theory of crises. She contended that such theories lacked a foundation in reality and represented deterministic wishful thinking, rather than a serious analysis of the capitalist world crisis. In a text with a title that rather pointedly referred to him as 'another theoretician of collapse' (*'Ein neuer Zusammenbruchstheoretiker'*), she accorded Grossman's theory very little credibility.

'For Henrik Grossmann, as well as Rosa Luxemburg, the proposition that capitalism must invariably experience internal bankruptcy is the most significant component of scientific socialism'. However, while Rosa Luxemburg wanted to prove this thesis first in order to fill an alleged gap in Marxism Grossman believes 'that the progress of Marxian research consisted and could only consist in the necessity of the downfall of capitalism through purely economic argumentation, to show it from the analysis of the capitalist system itself'.[1] Natalie Moszkowska challenged Grossman's theory of collapse by highlighting a key aspect of late capitalism, which she referred to as the 'Capitalism of our time'. She noted that the crises typically seen in this era often lead to protracted depressions. These economic downturns, she argued, do not necessarily result in the complete collapse of capitalism, but rather usher in prolonged periods of widespread impoverishment. In her analysis, this translated into a gradual increase in real wages, albeit not at a pace commensurate with the rise in productivity.[2] In her 1931 work, 'Criticism of Modern Crisis Theories', Natalie Moszkowska elucidated a dynamic in which crisis-ridden capitalism sought to address its challenges by resorting to the war economy of fascism as a method to overcome its difficulties – a perspective similar to that of Helene Bauer.

1 Bauer 1929, pp. 270–1.
2 Moszkowska 1931.

In her own 1931 publication titled 'On the Crisis in the World-Economy', Helene Bauer identified monopoly capitalism as one of the underlying causes of the global crisis of the 1930s. Historically, many had believed that the rapid resolution of post-war crises could be achieved through the trend of establishing monopolies and cartels, seen as mechanisms to reduce economic anarchy. However, Helene Bauer held a contrasting view, seeing monopolies as a force that exacerbated economic anarchy. She posited that cartels were more inclined to resist market forces compared to sole proprietorships. In this light, she doubted their willingness to embrace any form of 'order' that would enhance market competition. This stance rendered them anti-social even within the framework of market capitalism.

But, is it not a mistake to assume that capitalist enterprises with monopoly-like power would introduce a new, regulating, planned economy element into the struggles for the market? A planned economy coordinates the divergent, it is the concordance of diversity condensed into one purpose. A monopoly, however, is much more stubborn, much more 'anti-social' than an individual entrepreneur on whom the competition imposes the law of the market at all times: the monopoly fuels the resistance to the necessary adjustment to the market and is therefore directed against everyone.[3]

Helene Bauer pointed to the final period of economic upswing in the 1920s, during which monopolies demonstrated their ability to evade market pressures. This evasion intensified the strain on all other components of the economy and deepened the disparities within various sectors. In essence, the anarchy within the economy reached its zenith under the influence of monopoly capitalism within the context of global economic interdependence through exchange. A similar conclusion can be found in Adolf Strumthal's book *The Great Crisis*, published in 1937. Strumthal, a close associate of Friedrich Adler, managed to immigrate to the United States to escape Nazi persecution, where he continued his work on crisis theory and the consequences of the profound crisis in Europe.

> The differences in the social and economic situation of the producers, and the differences in market dominance that arise from them, were reflected in the last upswing period, in an uneven, anarchic price development; until finally, the plight of the many millions of peasant economies and the inhibited growth of the manufactured goods industry became a dam that halted the flow of profits of the monopoly industries.[4]

---

3 Bauer 1931, p. 123.
4 Bauer 1931, p. 124.

In 1932, a year after composing her treatise on the impact of monopolies on the crisis, Helene Bauer came to a profound realisation about the calamitous consequences of the crisis, not only on the global economy but also on the standing of social democracy and the workers' movement in Europe. She recognised that the masses were holding the socialist governments, where they had a share in power, responsible for the hardships inflicted by the crisis. The general public, largely unaware of the crisis's global nature and its far-reaching consequences, attributed their suffering to these socialist governments.

> However, the mere fact that, at the onset of the current crisis, socialist labels adorned the governments of both countries was sufficient to make the masses perceive the two workers' parties (England and Germany) as jointly responsible for everything they were too weak to prevent. Consequently, the crisis led to electoral defeats for them, the loss of their previous parliamentary positions, and soon rendered them powerless in the face of the system that they had recently criticised, denied, but seemed to shield and protect with the names of their leaders.[5]

During the 1930s, the most prevalent strategies for overcoming the financial crisis were twofold. First, there was a focus on fortifying the internal market, which entailed the establishment of economic autarchy and the imposition of protective tariffs on imported goods. The second approach involved the implementation of austerity measures, akin to the way neoclassical economic doctrine addresses contemporary financial crises. Helene Bauer staunchly opposed both austerity measures and import restrictions. She comprehended that international trade did not create a zero-sum game, and neither did internal spending. She was acutely aware that for economic prosperity to be maintained, someone had to spend, so that others can save. Concerning Austria, she noted: 'No state can artificially suppress imports without damaging foreign exports', and '[t]he decrease in exports took place here at an even faster pace than the decrease in imports, and the decrease in the foreign trade volume is accompanied by a constant increase in the unemployment rate!'[6]

Helene Bauer's critique of austerity measures appears remarkably relevant even today. This resonance is partly due to the recurrence of the same liberal fiscal orthodoxy, which was employed to address the crisis in the early 1930s and proved ineffective. Strikingly, this same austerity strategy continues to have a

5 Bauer 1932, p. 495.
6 Ibid.

detrimental impact on Europe in the present day, contributing to comparable social and political damage over the long term. Mark Blythe's commentary on the current crisis and the inefficacy of austerity measures in resolving it bears a striking resemblance to Helene Bauer's evaluation of these very measures in the 1930s. This highlights the enduring debate surrounding austerity policies and their implications for economic and social well-being.

We tend to forget that someone has to spend for someone else to save; otherwise, the saver would have no income from which to save. This problem is especially pernicious under a policy of generalized austerity because if the country's private and public sectors are both paying back debt at the same time (deleveraging), then the only way that country can grow is by exporting more, preferably with a lower exchange rate, to a state that is still spending. But it becomes self-defeating if everyone is trying the same strategy of not spending, as is happening in Europe today.[7]

In the early 1930s, Germany adopted the same self-defeating strategy of austerity as a response to the crisis. The vivid memories of the hyperinflation of 1919–1923 had a profound influence on the German populace, leading to strong opposition against the idea of 'credit expansion' and countercyclical investments. In contrast to the later beneficial approaches championed by figures like John Maynard Keynes and Franklin Delano Roosevelt, who advocated massive inflation-backed public investments, the German response involved a reduction in the price level and wages. The aim was to restore economic competitiveness. This strategy, known as deflation, was, and still is, an integral part of the politics of general austerity. Interestingly, in 1932, both Marxist and orthodox economists came to an unusual agreement about cutting back on spending and lowering prices – austerity and deflation. Both of them saw them as the best way out of the crisis.

Rudolf Hilferding, an Austromarxist and the Minister of Finances in the Weimar Republic, advocated for austerity and fiscal orthodoxy, opposing the Keynesian approach put forth by Wladimir Woytinsky, who proposed credit-backed public works as a remedy for the crisis. Hilferding's rejection of Keynesianism was influenced not only by the fear of another bout of hyperinflation but, according to Engelbert Stockhammer, was more fundamentally driven by a suspicion that its success would undermine the Marxist labour theory of value. What's intriguing is that Adolf Hitler adopted Woytinsky's approach, using it as a central part of his platform and achieving a resounding electoral victory over the socialists, primarily due to his promise to end austerity.

7 Blythe 2013, p. 9.

In 1930, Hans Zeisl, a young socialist sociologist who was involved in the renowned Marienthal unemployment research alongside Paul Lazarsfeld and Marie Jahoda, raised concerns about the limitations of adhering to the labour theory of value. He argued that this theory couldn't adequately account for the complexity of modern economic relations and posed a challenge to the overall socialist strategy, especially in terms of crisis and recession management. Unfortunately, his warnings went largely unheeded by the majority of influential socialist politicians.

When Franklin D. Roosevelt assumed office in 1932, Helene Bauer was unaware of the ultimate impact of his major investment plan. Consequently, she held reservations, fearing it might be yet another extension of Hoover's policies. It's important to note that John Maynard Keynes' seminal work, the *General Theory of Employment, Interest, and Money*, had not been published at that time; it was released in 1936.

Unlike Hiferding, Helene Bauer's criticism of Hoover's credit expansion policies wasn't rooted in opposition to credit and spending strategies in general. Instead, her critique centred on the direction in the investment of credit reserves. She was concerned that the primary beneficiaries of these policies were the stock market and large financial institutions, rather than efforts aimed at increasing employment and benefiting the broader population. 'In the fight against the crisis, enormous credit reserves were mobilised under Hoover's leadership. But the economy to which they were directed was only the stock market, and the disaster they now helped avert was not unemployment but the general bank crash'.[8]

Helene Bauer took into consideration the challenging circumstances imposed on Germany by the United States, stemming from the economic crisis in the U.S., particularly concerning the matter of reparations. It would subsequently become evident that this issue proved to be one of the most contentious and divisive aspects during the 1932 elections. Adolf Hitler seized upon this issue and emerged victorious in the elections, capitalising on the widespread discontent surrounding reparations and leveraging it for his political gain.

The concessions made in the war debt issue, which the Union, as a creditor, is forced to grant to its debtors, lose their provisional character as the crisis persisted. And all the states that up until the Hoover Moratorium essentially only passed on the funds received from Germany through America, now demand, following the Lausanne Agreement, further payment deferrals and a renego-

8 Bauer 1932, p. 496.

tiation of debt obligations for themselves as well. The intricate structure of international war debt payment is on the verge of collapse.[9]

Helene Bauer firmly believed that conventional economics was incapable of providing a suitable solution to the ongoing crisis. Her conclusions resonate as a cautionary note in our contemporary era, where neoclassical financial remedies are once again being sought to address crises in Europe and beyond. Her insights serve as a reminder of the limitations of traditional economic approaches in the face of complex and persistent economic challenges.

'However, behind all the hollow busyness that harasses where it pretends to lead and assist, there lies a thought: not to let the capitalist system perish beneath the ruins of the capitalist economy – to persevere for the benefit of all those who still govern us even in the fourth winter of crisis. The system that privileges private ownership is to be saved, even though everything that could once be interpreted as its historical mission has long become outdated, even though everything that once envisioned by its ideologues is devalued and torn apart'.[10]

2 On Fascist Economy

Published in 1936, 'The Economic Upswing of Fascism' (original title: '*Konjunktur Aufschwung des Faschismus*'), stands as the final full-length article that Helene Bauer authored in the German language. During the time of writing, she was already in exile in Prague, having fled there following the Austrian Civil War in February 1934 and the takeover of the state by the Austrofascists under the leadership of Engelbert Dollfuss. Consequently, her last work was dedicated to comprehending the economic crisis as the backdrop for the ascent of fascist regimes.

Fascism, wherever it emerged, initially targeted and violently suppressed the organised labour movement. As history has shown, it later extended its hostilities towards liberal society and democracy in general, ultimately establishing authoritarian states that contributed to the outbreak of a new world war. Given this context, it is not surprising that the organised labour movement and leftist intellectuals were among the first to conduct comprehensive analyses of fascism, examining the mechanisms through which it gradually seized power and the societal and economic conditions that facilitated its rise. In contrast, lib-

9 Bauer 1932, p. 497.
10 Bauer 1932, p. 499.

eral intellectuals only began addressing fascism much later, after the fascist and national socialist regimes had already wreaked havoc in Europe. For many of them, fascism was of little interest until World War II began. However, for some, like Ludwig Mises, fascism was a welcome and long-anticipated force that promised to forcibly quash the organised labour movement.

Among the early intellectuals who provided detailed analyses of fascism were German, Austrian, and Italian thinkers, including Helene and Otto Bauer. Otto Bauer, for instance, attributed the rise of fascism in Italy to a combination of concrete historical factors and players. These factors included militarism following World War I, the demobilisation and reintegration of war veterans in Italy, the financial crises and inflation that weakened the bourgeoisie in Germany and Austria, and the 1929 stock market crash and the ensuing global economic crisis. German thinker August Thalheimer and Italian intellectual Angelo Tasca also adopted similar analytical approaches. Thalheimer began outlining his theory of fascism in 1928, focusing on the relationship between the class position of the petty bourgeoisie and the structures and content of fascist ideology. He drew parallels between the rise of fascism and the historical emergence of Bonapartism under Louis Bonaparte.[11] On the other hand, Angelo Tasca concentrated his attention on concrete players rather than causalities.[12] In his final article penned in 1938, Otto Bauer departed from his previous perspective, which had depicted fascism as a manifestation of Bonapartism, in favour of forging a more intimate link between fascism and imperialism.[13]

Helene Bauer, on the other hand, identified the global economic crisis as the primary catalyst for the ascension of fascism to power. Her focus was on the economic conditions that precipitated a shift in power from the socialists to the fascists. The worldwide economic crisis brought about significant alterations in the structure of the global economy. Agricultural nations turned to industrialisation to meet their own needs, as credit tightened and import tariffs on commodities increased. Meanwhile, industries in established European economies contracted. This economic upheaval played a pivotal role in the rise of fascism. 'The state had to intervene in the economies – that had become necessary under the pressure of the crisis since long-term loans for investment purposes were unavailable. The state became a refuge'.[14]

11 Thalheimer 1930.
12 Tasca 1950.
13 I elaborated on this thesis in more detail in 'Imperialism in Austromarxism', forthcoming in Historical Materialism Special Edition on Austromarxism.
14 Bauer 1936, pp. 470–1.

Helene Bauer explained that the rise of an all-powerful state, a hallmark of fascism, was a response to the perceived need for centralised economic direction to overcome the severe recession. She was a strong critic of laissez-faire economic policies. However, even in 1936, she cautioned against embracing state interventionism and excessive statism as a panacea for the crises afflicting the global capitalist economy. Her perspective was rooted in a nuanced understanding of the complex economic and political forces at play during that period.

'The state interventions in the economy created a war of all against all on an external level, which was (additionally) burdened with a general currency uncertainty since the devaluation of the pound and the dollar and a bureaucratic, more-less haphazard management of the economy by the state, which in Italy and Germany, in two fascist great powers with now again a high level of employment, turned into a transformation and finally domination of the economy by the state'.[15]

She proceeded to elucidate the fundamental distinction between the state-run economies of national-socialist Germany and fascist Italy, as well as the state intervention in the economy that she had observed in smaller state-run economies.

'The economy of a fascist superpower bears entirely different characteristics from statism, from the isolated, uncoordinated, and mostly day-to-day improvised state interventions in the small countries oscillating between parliamentarism and dictatorship. The fascist dictatorship of the superpower aims to suppress and subdue social tensions through an imperialistic ideology, brand class strugglers as traitors to the state, and therefore must program revenge, war, and conquest as the purposes of the state'.[16]

In Mussolini's 1932 text 'The Doctrine of Fascism', which was written under Giovanni Gentile's guidance, he emphasised the importance of state intervention in the economy and the abandonment of laissez-faire policies. Although Mussolini cited Keynes as one of his economic references, his state-controlled economy differed significantly from the Keynesian model. It was not an economy geared toward achieving full employment for the benefit of public and social prosperity, but rather an economy oriented towards war and conquest. Helene Bauer was acutely aware of this fundamental aspect of the fascist economy under Mussolini's regime.

'This was followed by a period of extreme exploitation of foreign credit, and when the pump economy came to an end due to creditor rebellion, nearly the

15 Bauer 1936, p. 471.
16 Ibid.

entire gold reserve was sacrificed to the industrialisation of the country, which had already begun to clearly serve the purposes of armament and war preparation. Through rapidly succeeding domestic loans, the state absorbed all newly accumulated funds in the country, until eventually, through the nationalisation of central banks, the credit system became a branch of public administration'.[17]

Helene Bauer viewed the state-controlled economy in Nazi Germany through a similar lens. Just like Mussolini's Italy, Hitler's Germany operated its economy in a dictatorial manner, primarily to achieve maximum preparedness for war. The state resorted to compulsory borrowing from financial institutions and prohibited private share issuances to obtain liquid funds from the market. These funds were then allocated to industries of paramount national significance, while less critical sectors were constrained through investment restrictions, startup bans, and expansion prohibitions. This approach underscored the prioritisation of the war effort within the national-socialist economy.

The state-run economy of fascism created mass employment through low payment, which ended the recession, but only for the sake of war and expansion. The cheaper and more abundant standard of living, towards which the former German foreign trade aspired, has been replaced by the state leadership and 'the struggle for costly self-sufficiency that was imposed on the economy, which is supposed to enable perseverance in a war with an uncertain front and even more uncertain allies'.[18]

While certain sectors of their industries were thriving, and the unemployment rates were lower than in 1929, Helene Bauer discerned that these states were not experiencing a resurgence of capitalism. Instead, they were operating within a fascist economic system that was in full swing. This system was marked by a growing scarcity of food and essential resources, as well as low-wage labour, revealing the complex dynamics of these regimes. 'Disenfranchised workers make feverish preparations for war and perseverance'.[19] This is how fascism reversed the global economic downturn by employing Keynesian macro-economic tactics to fuel the war machine, which was destined to destroy Europe.

---

17 Ibid.

18 Bauer 1936, p. 472.

19 Bauer 1936, p. 473.

CHAPTER 8

Marriage, Emancipation and Social Class

The modern family's history begins with the history of the modern nation-state in the nineteenth century. The core family, which presupposes only the mother, father and their children living under the same roof, became predominant with the victories the bourgeoisie won against the feudal system. Previously in feudalism, most people, above all peasants, lived for centuries in greater families, where different generations lived together due to the objective constraints tied to their position of dependency on landlords and labour-intensive, low-productivity agriculture. On the other hand, the scarce city dwellers lived on trade and craftsmanship, which allowed for different family structures reminiscent of the bourgeois model of the nineteenth century and beyond.

The advent of industrialisation precipitated a significant transformation in economic structures and labour dynamics. The initial wave of industrial workers found themselves straddling two worlds: one foot in agriculture and the other as wage-earning labourers in burgeoning industries. However, the exigencies of industrial growth, including the clustering of factories near resource-rich areas and the swell in the overall population, compelled a massive migration of workers from rural to industrial hubs, where their livelihoods became entirely dependent on wages. This shift gave rise to alterations in social stratification and family configurations. During this period, both the archetypal bourgeois family and the proletarian family became nuclear families. Nevertheless, the distinctions between these two family models were profound. The bourgeois family, which had evolved as a historical construct within the urban milieu of late feudalism, had now solidified its place as a foundational element of society, embraced by the philosophies of late nineteenth-century Liberalism and Romanticism. In stark contrast, the proletarian family, functioning as a nuclear family, was a product of sheer necessity and external circumstances.

The nineteenth century marked a pivotal era during which both the nation and the modern state were forged. This transformative historical process, instrumental in globalising the nation-state paradigm, found its tangible expression in the wake of the late-eighteenth century American and French revolutions. At its core, this momentous transformation was defined by a profound shift in the conception of sovereignty, transitioning from the traditional notion vested in 'the house of the ruler' to a novel conception grounded in the sovereignty of the people.

This transformation engendered two fundamental questions of paramount importance in the realm of political theory. It necessitated the definition of the people as the constitutive entity in which sovereignty ultimately resided. Simultaneously, it raised inquiries into the dimensions of popular sovereignty, demarcated by the institutional and legal constraints delineating the boundaries of popular influence on decision-making and execution. The advent of the modern nation-state further mandated the introduction of universal suffrage for men, culminating in the establishment of a collective popular will.

The German model of the nation-state, in stark contrast to the French model rooted exclusively in political Liberalism, bore the heavy influence of Romanticism. This ideological perspective did not envision the state as a society wherein individuals come together within a structured framework, forming institutions that represent their individual or group interests. Instead, it perceived the state as a living organism, wherein distinct social strata functioned as different constituent organs. Within this framework, each social class – whether farmers, labourers, the aristocracy, or the bourgeoisie – was intricately interwoven as integral components of this biologically conceived organism, which was perceived as unchanging. This ideological stance facilitated an ostensibly improbable amalgamation of the modern nation-state and the existing feudal social structures, resulting in a harmonious coexistence of bourgeois and feudal systems epitomised by the German Imperial State. The same ideology served as the blueprint for the subsequent construction of the fascist corporate state, known as the '*Ständesstaat*'.

The emergence of the nation-state and the associated question of sovereignty vested in the people raised further questions regarding the definition of nationhood. Nationalism, serving as the ideological glue that unified a diverse population into a distinct and cohesive group, relied on shared but imagined common foundations, including religion, religious affiliation, a common language, and a presumed shared culture. The myth of the nation, combined with the simultaneous proliferation of nation-state formation throughout the Western world, ushered in a new set of moral and legal concepts. Among these, the family assumed a pivotal role. In the early Liberal tradition, individuals were regarded as the fundamental units of society. However, with the ascendance of the structured nation-state, this foundational unit transformed into a core family, representing an integral and essential constituent of the new state. Within this family framework, the father, perceived as the breadwinner, assumed a position of sovereign authority within the family and extended this authority beyond it and into the state.

This concept of an organic unity between God, the state, and the family was most comprehensively expounded by G.F.W. Hegel. In his philosophical framework, the will of God is mirrored in the state and, from there, permeates the family. This ideal-typical model was tailored to fit the ideal-typical bourgeois family and the modern nation-state. It established the notion that a man should serve as the breadwinner, while a 'good woman' should refrain from meddling in the social and economic sphere. Instead, she was expected to fulfill her 'natural' role, which was redefined in the nineteenth century as a threefold duty: wife, mother, and housewife. However, this 'ideal' model owed more of to myth, idealisation, and wishful thinking than the reality of actual capitalist society. For the vast majority of women in the nineteenth century, encompassing peasants, proletarians, small craftspeople, and even the aristocracy (alongside their husbands), the reality was vastly different from this idealised model.

Peasant women typically lived within extended families and their responsibilities included a wide range of tasks, such as tending to animals, milking, fermenting dairy products, agricultural work, and even selling agricultural produce. Childcare was generally a collective effort, with older women in the extended family playing a significant role. Consequently, the prescribed threefold role envisioned by bourgeois philosophers was largely inapplicable to this type of family structure. In the case of proletarian families, their economic circumstances were so dire that relying solely on the father's wage was insufficient for survival. Women and children were compelled to join the workforce, and it was not uncommon for children as young as four years old to be employed in mining and textile industries. In stark contrast to men, women worked as day labourers without any job security or even basic workers' rights. Their wages were often only half or even two-thirds of what men earned; the perception of women and children as 'unfair competition' frequently led to conflicts within the earliest organised labour unions.[1]

In these circumstances, the threefold role of a woman imagined by the liberal national philosophers was a reality only within the small circle of the new industrial bourgeoisie. The women living on small crafts or small trade run by their husbands were deeply incorporated in their businesses: 'The labour-power of the woman is here to such a high degree a condition of the economic existence of the family and supplementing the man's employment that in the merging of gender and economic community, civil marriage becomes a social structure like the rural one, whose dissolution destroys or cripples something organic'.[2]

1 Lange and Bäumer 1902, p. 398.
2 Bauer 1927 C, pp. 320–1.

While Hegel and other bourgeois philosophers constructed marriage as an idealised category that aligned with their desires and the circumstances of the limited social strata of the emerging bourgeoisie, Helene Bauer recognised that the economic underpinnings of marriage varied across different social classes. She understood that economic survival necessitated different forms of marriage within the capitalist system, resulting in a multitude of marriage types coexisting in reality.

> "The economic landscape of the present, which we designate with the term 'capitalism', is richly structured into a juxtaposition and intermingling of old, new, and newest forms, which also coexist as a colourful mixture of cultural spheres even in the smallest nation-states. From this diversity of socio-economic foundations arises a diversity of ways of life, and consequently, a diversity of marriages that strongly vary in their meaning and content, but all still must be counted as part of the 'today'."[3]

The first movements for the emancipation of women surged from the bourgeoisie in which women indeed lived according to Hegel's model – in other words, entirely economically dependent on a husband in a way that no other social class of the epoch was. They urged for political suffrage, equal rights within the marriage and access to high education and the legal right to gainful employment. With the rise of the workers' movement, the first socialist women movements emerged too, fighting to improve working conditions and achieve equal salaries and social benefits. The first quests for an equal right to gainful employment came up in the United Kingdom in the middle of the nineteenth century. They were sparked by the book *Women and Work* written by Barbara Bodichon followed by the book written by famous political philosopher John Stuart Mill and his wife Harriet Taylor Mill in 1867 in which they criticised the three-fold role the bourgeois society regarded as a 'natural' for women. As a British House of Commons member, John Stuart Mill filed the first motion for universal suffrage for women, which expectedly failed. He connected the necessity of women's liberation with his general theory of liberty.

At the time Helene Bauer wrote her work on the social stratification of marriage within the framework of industrial capitalism, she was among the relatively few theoreticians who dared to deviate from the idealised concepts of the core family perpetuated by bourgeois patriarchy. Another forerunner was Rosa Mayreder. Bourgeois philosophers, however, were not lonely in defending this imagined model that impeded every attempt to improve the circumstances of

3 Bauer 1927 C, p. 319.

women and children among the proletariat. Most first- and second-generation socialists also regarded women's professional work as a deviation and unfair competition to men.

Women working in low-wage industries faced challenges related to their work and social rights. These rights were intricately linked to their political rights. This shared concern over political rights extended not only to working-class women but also to bourgeois women who were dissatisfied with the limited roles assigned to them as dependent housewives. Consequently, the struggle for equal access to higher education became a central and unifying cause for women from various social backgrounds.

'Before the war, higher education for women was still a rarity – the impoverishment of the middle class due to the war and inflation has turned higher education for women, leading to independent earning, into a widespread phenomenon'.[4] This gave rise to a new kind of woman who was economically independent and self-aware. These women also challenged the traditional economic model of marriage.

> In the social sphere, a new type of marriage is added to the ones that already exist: the intellectually and economically independent woman is directly rooted in society and assumes obligations towards it, in which the man no longer shares. She represents only herself outwardly. The more opportunities are provided for her to satisfy her creative work drive outside the home, the less significant a role marriage may play in her life plan. Instead of adjusting her life to her marriage, she will now strive to adapt her marriage to a life that has shifted its focus outward.[5]

From the perspective of young bourgeois women's rights activists, who aimed to secure political rights and access to higher education, their own struggle for emancipation through education appeared even more complex than that of working-class women.

> On this point (education), the aspirations of proletarian and bourgeois women meet, the only difference being that the men of their circles support the former because they have the same demands to make, while the latter have to persuade their fathers and brothers to accept them.[6]

4 Bauer 1927c, p. 322.
5 Ibid.
6 Lange/Bäumer 1902, p. 163.

These lines make it evident that bourgeois feminists were already aware of the support from the Socialist Party and its workers' associations for women's emancipation. By the 1900s, the majority of the members of the Second International already endorsed women's emancipation, although there was a long and contentious path to reach this consensus, as the positions of male Socialists were divided on the issue for some time. Especially Ferdinand Lassalle, the founder of the General German Workers Union, was a vociferous adversary of women's emancipation, sharing entirely the patriarchal bourgeoisie views on women. 'In addition to the serious public family duties of the husband and father, the wife and mother should represent the cosiness of the poetry of domestic life, bring grace and beauty into social interactions and increase the enjoyment of the life of mankind in an ennobling way'.[7] It was thanks to the adamancy of Clara Zetkin that the Second Socialist International finally revisited its former stance influenced by Lassalle and decided to support the women's right to gainful employment officially at its congress in Paris in 1889. Zetkin resorted to the work of the popular socialist August Bebel, who supported women's economic and social independence as part and parcel of Socialism as did Emil Reich in Austria. For Clara Zetkin, the question of women's emancipation was inextricably interwoven with the emancipation of the working class in general. From 1889 onward, the emancipation of women became part of a program of socialist parties around Europe. Still, an equal position of women within socialist parties in Europe had a rocky way to go. Dorothy Thurtle commented on the Labour Party as late as 1930 that women are needed only if they have no opinion of their own, and French Socialist Germaine Picard-Moch lamented that the socialist men often behave as if there were no socialist women.[8] However, only Socialist and Communist parties regarded women as equal party members in the 1920s and 1930s. Already in 1914 German Socialist party had appoximately 175, 000 female members, and Clara Zetkin and Rosa Luxemburg were among the party leaders. Clara Zetkin became the Head of the Socialist International Women in 1907, which fought against militarism and for the inclusion of women in international workers' solidarity networks.[9]

In Austria, socialist women also had to fight against legal obstacles. The law of the Austrian Hungarian Empire forbade women's membership in political parties. Socialist women had to organise themselves on the fringes of the official Party in the form of 'educational sections'. The first was founded in 1890 at

7 Anderson and Zinsser 1988, p. 451.
8 Anderson and Zinsser 1988, p. 480.
9 Linzer Konferenz 1978, p. 183.

the initiative of Viktoria Kofler snd Adelheid Popp, a year after the Social Democratic Workers Party of Austria was founded in Hainfeld. Women gained the right to organise politically with the First Republic in 1918. Except for the Communists and left Social Democrats, all other parties did their best to reverse the process of both the political organisation of women and their right to gainful employment.[10] After 1918 the SDWP had by far the highest number of female parliament members. Out of 72 Socialist members of Parliament, nine were women in 1919: Adelheid Popp, Therese Schlesinger, Gabriele Proft, Emmy Freundlich, Amalie Seidl, Marie Tusch, Anna Boschek, Julie Rauscher, and Irene Sponner.[11] While the Social Democrats granted women the right to vote during their legislative period in 1919, the subsequent election in 1920 revealed that women in Austria predominantly voted for the Christian Socials, rather than the Social Democrats who had initially extended suffrage to them. This outcome was unexpected for both the Social Democrats and the Christian Socials. Therese Schlesinger dedicated an article in *Kampf* to analysis of this riddle.[12] Therese Schlesinger was an early associate of Augusta Flickert, a trailblazer in the early feminist movement, who maintained connections with August Bebel, a prominent German socialist and advocate of women's rights. While Flickert is often associated with bourgeois feminism, recent historical research has revealed that the boundaries between so-called bourgeois and socialist feminism were not as distinct as previously assumed. Flickert found the conservatism of the Christian Socials and the hypocrisy of the Liberals objectionable, and she held the Social Democrats in high regard.[13] Nevertheless, she never wanted to be associated with any political party.

Adelheid Popp and Therese Schlesinger were among the first generation of socialist feminists in Austria. Therese Schlesinger played a pivotal role in introducing the concept of deprivatising care and household duties, an idea that would later be developed by both Otto and Helene Bauer. This idea found its way into Helene Bauer's text on 'Marriage and Social Stratification' (in the appendix) and Otto Bauer's work on *'Mieterschutz, Volkskultur und Alkoholismus'*. The notion of deprivatising care and household duties was highly controversial during that period. Therese Schlesinger recognised that the lives of most women, except those from the upper classes, were consumed by caring for children, the elderly, and household chores. For women engaged in gainful employment, this burden was even greater. The most effective and rational

10 Lösch 1985; Schneider 2008.
11 Hauch 1995.
12 Schlesinger 1921.
13 Kulka 1919, p. 207.

solution was the socialisation of care and household work. Schlesinger envisioned the new municipal housing projects of 'Red Vienna' as a practical means to implement these ideas. She foresaw kindergartens, schools, and playrooms in every municipal housing project as a way to socialise childcare and relieve women of this responsibility. Furthermore, municipal housing should incorporate large communal kitchens and laundry services, which would be covered as part of the rental fee, thus deprivatising household work and further lightening the load on individual women. Community-based municipal living was seen as a more efficient and rational way of organising life.[14]

Helene Bauer would go a step beyond Therese Schlesinger, for she hoped that the future would bring a complete socialisation of care and household work, which would also radically change the future shape of marriage and family. 'This marriage has not yet found its form – but its content is already recognisable: it is an erotic comradely bond between equals, the only purpose of which can be the increase in the value of life'.[15] For Helene Bauer, such future marriage would already be dissolved in reality if just one of the partners no longer wanted it, and there would be no one whose protection would require the formal maintenance of such a relationship from the state authority. 'Here, just like the man, the woman is not thrown out of a home that means the world to her by divorce; she doesn't lose her place of work and influence, nor her social status, and she can remain an unburdened mother despite an unhappy marriage – unless she prefers to entrust the children to a communal upbringing'.[16]

Here again, we encounter the idea of the socialisation in the form of the socialisation of care. Socialisation in all its aspects was the most radical idea Austromarxism brought forward in the 1920s. It failed due to a conservative backlash to both its economic and social programs. It displayed, however, an unprecedented will to break the bondage of tradition and to re-think the system of beliefs that was presented as 'natural' for centuries – the sanctity of the traditional family as the only right environment for raising the children. The Austromarxists of the 1920s were characterised by a profound willingness to initiate radical and comprehensive societal transformations, a stance that was more pronounced during their time than it is in the twenty-first century. Like all Marxists, the Austromarxists were firm believers in the concept of progress, anticipating that the future would inevitably bring about positive change and emancipation. However, history has shown that these expectations were not always realised. Nonetheless, if we measure progress in terms of the willingness

14 Schlesinger 1925.

15 Bauer 1927 C, p. 322.

16 Bauer 1927 C, pp. 322–3.

to challenge and change deeply entrenched societal norms and to experiment with radical social innovations aimed at enhancing the lives of the majority of people, then Marxists and, more specifically, the Austromarxists, can be seen as among the most progressive forces in human history. This level of progressiveness finds parallels in the Renaissance period and the early era of political Liberalism.

Austromarxist female activists were particularly concerned with finding new alternative models of rational and sustainable living, which entailed a drastic reduction of individual household work. These ideas were implemented in the so-called 'one kitchen house' projects of socialised municipal housing. One such project was established in the municipal house in Pilgerimgasse in Vienna. A journalist and a tenant in this particular house, Bettina Hirsch, described the advantages of living in a house where all household work was socialised.

Hirsch described the house in Pilgerimgasse as a house, in which instead of more than 200 small kitchens, there was a large kitchen that prepared lunch and dinner at cost price. She emphasised that working women unable to keep domestic staff were given the opportunity to have a hot meal in their own home without having to use their short hours of rest for cooking and because large quantities were sourced, better quality and cheaper prices could be achieved than was possible with small-scale shopping. But the shared kitchen was not the only advantage of that system. The daily cleaning of our apartments was also taken care of by the house. This particular house had many other shared facilities: roof terraces, which were used for regular gymnastics in the early morning hours and offered sunbathing during the day with the showers installed there.

> We don't defend the one-kitchen house out of convenience. We defend it as the modern form of household that can embrace all technological achievements and therefore requires less and less human labour. We defend it as the means to bring about real equality for women, because only then can we really participate in the spiritual and cultural life of our time.[17]

All these amenities were affordable even for a single worker. Despite the evident advantages of the model described above, it would not assert itself in the 'Red Vienna' municipal buildings. The advent of fascism and, later, the annexa-

17 Hirsch, 1927.

tion to Hitler's Germany made an end to all such projects in Vienna. Even now, hundred years later a house as described by Bettina Hirsch appears more like a futuristic dream borrowed from the science fiction genre than as a reality that once existed in the city of Vienna.

PART 2

Writings of Helene Bauer

∵

CHAPTER 9

Bourgeoise and Socialist Economic Theory, *Der Kampf* (1926), Vol. 3: 63–8

Can there be a 'bourgeois' and a 'socialist' doctrine within the scope of economic theory if it is limited to establishing purely empirical facts, without the one necessarily being wrong if the other is correct? When asked what the economy should be like, different answers are, of course, possible depending on the political, social, and ethical standpoint of the person who answers; but can there be opposing answers to the question 'what is the economy' that are not based on either a lack of knowledge or wrong conclusions that yet seem to be mutually exclusive?

As far as the uncovering and representation of economic phenomena in their causal connections, the distance between Marx's economic teachings and those of bourgeois economists is, in fact, much shorter than is generally assumed. During the long period between the publication of the first volume of *Capital* and the third, (which, as we now know, does not conclude the system but rather contains its practical prerequisites) one could still justifiably doubt whether the abstract determinations of his theory of value have any validity in reality – that is, whether they will lead us to the concrete forms of modern economic life. However, the third volume offers us the capitalist world, with its own interest and profit calculations, the interplay of supply and demand, private calculations and market prices, and the interaction between the profit rate and the interest rate. It is a reflection of capitalist exchange processes in all their complicated interrelations, which ultimately always appear to be determined by the individual's pursuit of more profit or higher wages.[1] The image we see here is fundamentally shaped by empirical material and thus recurs in all economic theories; bourgeois economic theory, albeit through different paths,

1 'Introduction to a Contribution to the Critique of Political Economy', printed in: Marx, *Zur Kritik der politischen Ökonomie*. 2. Reprint. Stuttgart 1907. 'The concrete is concrete because it is the synthesis of many determinations, a unity of the diverse. In thought, it thus appears as a process of synthesis, as a result, not as a starting point, although it is the real starting point and therefore the actual starting point of perception and conception. In the first approach, the full conception is diluted into abstract determination; in the second, the abstract determinations lead to the reproduction of the concrete through the process of thought'. (Translated by the author)

also uncovers the same causal connections that subject the well-known 'isolated economic agent' of marginal utility to the laws of free competition.

The contribution that Marx's exploration of the capitalist world has made to the science of economics has neither been doubted nor subjected to serious criticism by bourgeois economists. For example, the way Marx raised the problem of capital accumulation and crises has been recognised, analysed, and placed at the centre of heated debates (almost exclusively by socialists) in terms of its significance for understanding the present. However, these technical issues, which undoubtedly belong to the essence of economics, failed to capture the attention of bourgeois theorists. They are fixated, as if spellbound, solely on Marx's 'labour theory of value', solely examining whether it 'agrees' with price. Never satisfied that it is truly dead, these bourgeois theorists attempt to bury it under entire mountains of value-theory debates, which often serve as substitutes for serious economic inquiry.

But is the rejection of Marx's labour theory of value really just about the significance of the concept of value in constructing the edifice of economic theory, about the selection and appreciation of the best methodological tools for accurately determining economically significant facts or economic development trends? Is Böhm-Bawerk's judgment of Marx's value theory – that it is 'reckless, premature presumption', 'false dialectic', 'internal contradiction', and 'blindness to facts' – really just the expression of a differing opinion on the cognitive value of various research methods, which could, through further refinement in theoretical work, testing against material, and comparing results, clarify and unify the development of the discipline? Or is there a fundamental discord here that reaches beyond what can be empirically researched and cannot be reconciled to a common denominator, even if the numerator is correct?[2]

Socialist economic theory views workers in their relationships with one another as members of a community characterised by division of labour, which it emphasises as the social world distinct from the rest of nature. 'It is the unique position, the exclusive value emphasis, which German idealist philosophy assigns to humans as willing subjects in contrast to objective nature, that reappears here in Marx, though in a form often veiled by naturalism, and allows him to imbue Ricardo's labour theory of value with a distinctly unique vitality'.[3]

---

2 Böhm-Bawerk. E.: Geschichte und Kritik der Kapitalzinstheorien. Innsbruck. 1900. Page 495–6.

3 Perth Fr.: Der soziale Gehalt der Marxschen Wertlehre. Jena. 1916. Page 18. Compare with the discussion that Hilferding dedicated to this beautiful and interesting work. Grunbergs Archiv fur die Geschichte des Sozialismus und der Arbeiterbewegung. Year 8, Volume 2 and 3. Leipzig 1919.

The soil, the treasures it holds within, forests and rivers, sun and rain – these are the natural conditions of human labour, just as labour itself is a natural force of the human organism, directed by reason and will. The tool that humans create, the machines of labour and power, join the relatively stable natural conditions of labour with new cultural conditions gained through experience, passed down from generation to generation as an ever-richer inheritance, increasing and multiplying the yield of labour. The worker harnesses natural forces, utilises the means of production created by human intellect, shapes the material – and what is produced is the worker's product, to which nature and culture have lent their resources.

In the attachment of humans to the material and the machine during the work process, a piece of human personality is bound, and this is given away with their work product. The exchange of work products thus means that all producers are drawn into the circle of exchange work for one another. Each one, in giving a part of their personality to a good that is meant to serve someone else, can only receive an equivalent value from the labour of others, which serves their own purposes with equal dedication. Only labour for labour now appears to be an exchange of similar and therefore comparable values. This exchange is only possible within the circle of working people who, through their labour, create various goods for one another, exchanging them either directly or indirectly through the mediation of money and the market, which informs each person whether their individual labour is actually useful to others and to what extent. *Anyone who does not belong to this circle does not possess an equivalent good for exchange and cannot possess one*, as such value can *only be gained through personal dedication*. They may demand their share in the form of interest, profit, or rent, and may gain control over the work product through the seizure of the natural conditions of labour; but within the larger community of workers, they will remain merely an outsider, confronting the value of personality with their ownership titles.

The labour process is always an interaction of humans with nature. However, in order to produce, people enter into certain relationships with one another and it is only within these social relations and conditions that their interaction with nature, as well as production and exchange, take place.[4] Under capitalist production relations, the labour process develops as an interaction of labour power – which the propertyless must sell in order to survive – with nature, monopolised in the hands of capitalists. The result is an exchange that, through the masked and often convoluted paths of modern market transactions, deliv-

4 Marx: Lohnarbeit und Kapital. Berlin 1891. Page 23.

ers a portion of the social product to the owners of the conditions of labour. For Marx, the study of the causal chain of these exchanges, the individual motivations of buyers and sellers, and the resistances that the social environment places against individual calculations – thereby producing outcomes at their intersections that no one had either intended or wanted – are not an end in themselves. Rather, they are merely a path through which he investigates the fate of labour, that is, the personality of the worker. The essential problem that his value theory raises is not which use-values individuals choose, or how they evaluate them within the limits of their purchasing power, but rather how much remains through the market to satisfy other social groups.

The struggle of bourgeois economic theory against Marx is focused on unraveling this problem. Marx's evaluative standpoint makes his theory independent of any results from practical economic research, turning it into a critique of political economy. This is why all scholars and practitioners who have no reason to be dissatisfied with the existing property order must perceive his theory as a constant threat to the world they cherish.

> Experience shows, above all, that the national product results from the cooperation of human labour with material means of production, which are partly of natural origin, partly artificial (land, capital), and is distributed according to some key to the parties that contribute these cooperating factors. If one holds the highly debatable opinion that only one of the actual participants should participate, so that the participation of others is, from the outset, an exploitation of that one, then one would have to look deeply into the internal relationship of these factors and try to demonstrate for internal reasons that, despite the external majority of cooperating factors, one of them alone, or at least for the purpose of distribution, means everything and therefore can claim everything for itself, leaving nothing for the others.[5]

Here, one of the most insightful representatives of marginal utility theory not only formulates the opposition between bourgeois and socialist economic theory with commendable openness, but also provides interpretations that reveal his own evaluative standpoint. The 'participants' in distribution are presented here as 'participants' in production—that is, as a majority of 'cooperating factors', who receive a share of the collectively produced whole in proportion to quotas, the laws of which remain to be studied. It is not the cultured human

---

5 Böhm-Bawerk E.: Page 550.

in their specific way of interacting with nature, but rather the human alongside the land and their tools – the human and the material world – that are recognised as original and equally valuable sources of value creation. These sources only temporarily merge their streams into a common bed, only to separate again. The recognition of the creative character of the material world, through which the distinctive bourgeois income types – wages, profit, rent – are traced back to equally distinct typical contributions from equally distinct typical participants, both erases the distinction between labour and ownership titles and forms the essence and content of bourgeois economic theory, regardless of whether its solutions seem more or less peculiar, insightful, or shallow.

We always see here 'cooperating factors' that are contributed to the collective work by parties who are initially denied access to the public stage by theory. The creative human thus appears as 'labour' – as an activity detached from humans and society, which always bear a historically determined character, and to which 'land' (as all of organic and inorganic nature) and 'capital' (as the technical apparatus of the economy at the current stage of material culture) are joined. Land, labour, and capital cooperate and create not only many useful and necessary things but also the modern bourgeois forms of income. For now, the owners, who had been relegated to the background by economic theory, emerge and claim the reward for the 'cooperation' of their factors: the worker, who had been there all along, and the capitalist and landowner, who appear for the final act. The key by which the total product is distributed is sought by the Marxist school in historically given power relations, while bourgeois theorists seek it in the importance of each 'factor' in bringing about the final product. Since labour cannot produce goods without material and yields only sparse results without tools, land, material, and tools are considered equally indispensable to production; from this perspective, land, tools, and material are just as productive and just as much a 'value' as labour. And thus the path is paved for all the theories of utility, performance, and productivity that attribute the origin of interest and rent to the natural qualities of the land and the technical development of tools.[6]

The theory of distribution, which emphasises the natural characteristics of things in order to obscure the question of social relations, requires a 'natural value' in which the relationship between humans is erased and replaced by evaluations through which humans confront things. 'Value' is what is desired, and the scale of values is determined by the intensity of the desire. What is 'rare' becomes more 'valuable' than what is considered common. Land, raw materi-

6 Compare: Marx, Capital. Vol. 3/2. Paragraph VII "The trinitarian equasion".

als, the means of production – everything that is owned by few and which can be completely withheld from others or only offered in limited quantities on the market – takes on a higher value in light of these theories. Meanwhile, human labour, which is urgently offered under the pressure of necessity, is regarded as a good that exists in uneconomic proportions compared to other goods and thus registers a correspondingly small 'natural' value. This 'natural value' then determines the equally natural price of labour, meaning the portion of the total product that can be 'attributed' to the workers, while the remaining amount is allocated by pure economic theory of the marginal value school to the owners.[7] Capitalist distribution is here transformed into a meaningful connection between value and price and the free play of economic forces into a mechanism that, with unsurpassed precision, is able to reward all contributing factors according to their value – that is, according to their importance in the production of goods. However, upon even superficial analysis, this importance is revealed to be the workers' plight, which forces them, depending on the market situation, to settle for higher or lower wages, with the share for profit and rent automatically rising or falling in the opposite direction independently the structure of the production process. Nevertheless, bourgeois economic theory examines the economy as an exchange system, not the social conditions that influence its course.

The formula 'to labour the wage – to land the rent, to capital the interest', in which labour, land, and capital are seen as the respective causes of wage, rent, and interest, does not yet offer everything that a proper bourgeois theory is obliged to provide.

The worker who receives wages offers personal effort and is easily identifiable as the cause. However, the connection between the productive contributions of land and capital, and the receipt of interest and rent, appears questionable if the power of ownership is not included as an explanatory factor in the theoretical investigation. However, bourgeois economic theory must not cross the conceptual threshold that leads from economics to the social realm, because the paths beyond it lead to a critique of political economy. What kind of relationship, then, can be established between the person of the capitalist and the landlord and the contributions, utilities, or productivity of the things they contribute to production? Here, there is an obvious gap. As such, bourgeois economic theory can only explain the various forms of bourgeois income, without revealing the class structure of modern society and the conflict of

7 Wieser: Theorie der gesellschaftlichen Wirtschaft. Grundriss der Sozialökonomik. 1. Chapter. Hamburg 1914.

interests between labour and ownership, if it succeeds in linking even the mere beneficiaries to the economy through an economic function.

The brazenly naïve abstinence theory of Senior, who found the justification for capital interest in the painful deprivations imposed on the rich in order to provide capital from their savings for productive purposes, was dismissed even by interest-friendly theorists as too crude and, in its crudeness, too provocative. Yet, Senior's problem and task remain the problem and task of bourgeois theoretical research, which has disavowed Senior but has remained unable to escape the confines of his solutions to this day.

In Marshall's theory of interest, 'the efforts directly or indirectly associated with the various types of labour necessary for the production of a good, and the abstinences, or better, sacrifices of waiting, which must be borne so that the capital required for the production of goods is saved: all these efforts and sacrifices together form the real production costs of the good in question', we find, heavily influenced by Senior, a few new variations of the old theory. Each of these, whether psychologically or market-based, was developed into a distinct theory of distribution, presented at some university as 'the theory that triumphed over Marx'.[8] The formulations place more emphasis on waiting (Cassel) in one case, and more on effort and sacrifice (Clark) in another, but the epistemological goal of all three schools remains the same: to reinterpret the capitalist's way of life, accumulation, as a personal achievement that demands compensation.

The sacrifice of waiting displaced the abstinence theory, but the crudeness of the new doctrine too closely resembles the shabby nature of the old for it to claim more than a small portion of the contested field in the struggle of ideas for a meaningful interpretation of unearned income. It is mostly mixed in a modest dose with various theories of utility and productivity, and in this blend, it also appears with Böhm-Bawerk – but in an artfully processed form, devoid of any trivial praise for the reconciling virtues of interest recipients. This casuistry seemingly aims to establish nothing but objective, that is, universally valid facts and relationships. In Böhm-Bawerk, the capitalist also 'waits', but not from the sacrifice of waiting; instead, the ripe fruit of interest falls into his lap from the weaving and working of time. For goods whose production costs labour and time, the worker receives his wages for the future good to which his labour is dedicated, already in the present, when his work begins. The value of his product lies in the future and is currently diminished by the time gap required for its completion because, despite their similarity, future needs and

8 Marshall: Volkswirtschaftslehre (Priniciples of Economics). Page. 351.

satisfaction are felt less vividly than present ones. Future enjoyment is merely valued in the present with a discount, and thus a worker can only obtain the value of his future product now with a discount – similarly, he receives only what his good is worth at present. With the approach of the maturity of enjoyment, the value of the good increases and ultimately surpasses the value of the wage by an increment that arises from the disparity between the valuation of present and future goods, at the sale 'leaving something behind that the capitalist can and may appropriate'.[9] Here, the interest problem is transferred from the economic to the physical realm on the wings of finely spun theoretical discussions of value. But even if we want to follow Böhm-Bawerk's flight, the question of what motives drive the two parties to make the peculiar exchange of the present for the future remains valid. The propertylessness of the proletarian and the economic superiority of the entrepreneur create the psychological conditions for this exchange in the same way: from the necessity of one arises the valuation of the present good 'wage', and from the satiety of the other arises the physical inclination to conclude exchanges by temporarily foregoing the present good 'wage payment', which leaves 'something behind by itself' in his hands. Böhm-Bawerk's capitalist retains the 'value increment' of foreign labour for himself because the worker, under the social pressure that weighs on him, is forced to forgo his own labour product until his social position plays into his hands.

Bourgeois economic theory attributes the income that each social group receives from bourgeois society to its respective contributions. In this attribution, evaluations of creation and ownership, of labour and waiting, of people and things converge, and every price is traced back to a 'value' or a 'function' (Schumpeter, Cassel). The decision made by the capitalist market regarding the level of prices also appears as the ultimate objective judgment for these evaluations, which are merely motivated, while socialist theory criticises it by unpacking the labour problem. Here, their paths diverge and will necessarily remain separated as long as the class distinction, which generates the need for the ideological glorification of the status quo in one case and the unveiling of this ideology in the other, is not overcome.

9 Böhm-Bawerk E: Page 603.

CHAPTER 10

Bankruptcy of Marginal Utility Theory (1924), Vol. 3: 105–13

> The annual labour of a people is the fund that provides it with all the means of enjoyment and all the comforts of life that it consumes annually ... The value added by the workers to the material breaks down into two parts: wages and profit ... Rent constitutes the first deduction from the products of labour applied to the land ... Every good rise or falls in value ... depending on whether it can be produced more easily or more difficultly, in other words, in relation to the amount of labour necessary for its production.

These statements, which now sound so socialist, were formulated by the most eminent representatives of bourgeois science at a time when the vulnerability of the 'working poor', as the working class was officially called in England during the time of Smith and Ricardo, still allowed the representatives of bourgeois economics to take both their theoretical conscience and bourgeois bias into account. We see both combined in them. Smith and Ricardo investigate labour as the source of value and at the same time subject it to a social 'law of nature' that constantly refers to starvation wages. They recognise in the capitalist market the command of creation and privation for some, and enjoyment for others, and close themselves off from the recognition of its historical conditioning. They openly expose the capitalist lawfulness of the distribution of the social product of labour and yet do not doubt that the bourgeois expediency of a social order in which, according to Malthus' claim, 'nature does not provide a place at the table for all' ensures its eternal existence.

The nonchalance with which bourgeois researchers left value-creating labour to the workings of a natural law acting against it was unpleasantly disrupted by history. The 'working poor' has become a class-conscious fighter who draws his best weapons from the scientific arsenal provided by Marx's critique of political economy, using the proud battle cry: 'Honour to labour', to expose and threaten the rights flowing from ownership. The class struggle turned the creators into a community bound by their creative work, and thus the mere theoretical recognition of the value of labour appeared as taking sides for labour against ownership. Now, the bourgeoisie lost their joy in the scientific legacy of Smith and Ricardo, which was taken up and critically developed by Marx and

Engels. The bourgeois science moved further and further away from the labour theory of value, until, buried under an avalanche of historical and descriptive details, every theoretical investigation into the social sources of private profit was abandoned. The 'phantoms' of theory were denounced until a new generation, within the framework of a new theory of value deemed suitable to serve as a protective wall for the bourgeoisie against the onslaught of socialist critique, raised vehement protests against the 'arduous labour' of economic historicism and demanded a new place for theory under the academic sun.

They asked for it, and it was soon and gladly granted! Because the new value theory, which was developed by three men at the same time, the Viennese Karl Menger,[1] the Frenchman Leon Walras,[2] and the American W.St. Jevons,[3] independently formulated, seemed called upon to make up for the mistakes of the classics by dethroning the work. She contrasts the individual, the detached and hence historically indeterminate 'isolated agent', with a given stock of goods. Her estimates are supposed to prove to us now that 'the level of satisfaction of needs and its changes are much more important than the amount of labour contained in the goods that result in this satisfaction of needs, and their changes', which, according to Smith, Ricardo, and the evil Marxists, determine value.[4] If he possesses many goods of a certain type, he will soon realise that they not only satisfy one need but, depending on the quantity of pieces, they fulfil various needs of different importance. Alternatively, if it's only one need, then it is satisfied to a greater or lesser extent. As the number of pieces increases, the significance he attaches to each additional unit diminishes. From a single unit taken from the stock, he will currently rely only on the satisfaction of the least important, basic need. Consequently, he will not attribute greater importance to any individual unit of that stock beyond what corresponds to the least important need – the 'marginal utility' of one unit among several, exchangeable units, which, according to Menger, determines its value, forming the basis of exchange value.

In the stock of goods of the isolated agent, there are also higher-order goods (such as land, labour services, tools, fertilisers, etc.) that do not possess immediate utility but, when combined in a technically appropriate manner, could serve in the distribution of consumer goods. As promises of future enjoyment, they would certainly not appear worthless to him, even though their value estima-

1 Karl Menger, *Grundsätze der Volkswirtschaftslehre*. 1871.

2 Leon Walras, *Élements d'economie politique pure*. 1874.

3 W.St. Jevons. *Theory of Political Economy*. 1871.

4 Schumpeter. *Dogmen- und Methodengeschichte. "Grundriss der Sozialökonomie"*. Tübingen 1914, 1. Abteilung, S. 118.

tion might require a longer physical process. He must raise the question here: what would the consequence of losing a single unit or part of the complementary group of production goods he possesses be? 'The shortfall in total output that occurs under these conditions remains the quantity of output on which the owner is dependent due to the possession of the respective subset, and thus provides the basis for its value'. (Menger)

The new doctrine seemed to meet all the requirements that the bourgeoisie – feeling itself in a defensive position due to social struggles – could impose on a social theory. In the self-contained economy oriented towards use-value, prices are derived from the value estimates of individuals based on the calculation of value. Such an economy dissolves the work of social individuals shaping their existence through technology in their struggle with nature into a condition of existence alongside technology and nature and simultaneously disintegrates human society into loosely related economic subjects. Class antagonisms and conflicts of interest disappear, and history becomes eternal again, just like in the time of Smith and Ricardo!

The marginal utility theory soon became the best antidote against Marxism and the sole official theory of value in universities. Now, the task was to develop the first major framework for a conceptual system that would derive the categories of modern exchange economy – wages, rent, profit – in their quantitative determinacy from the value estimations of the 'isolated agent', without encountering the contradiction between labour and ownership, which seemed so successfully reconciled in the persona of the 'isolated agent'.

The new doctrine now had the task of attributing the social distribution of goods to the same elements of satisfaction, usefulness, and quantity on which the marginal utility theory had been built – that is, to return to the logical connection between the starting point and the individual problems, and thereby conceptually grasp and present wages and profit as natural economic phenomena independent of historical power and dependency relations.

Menger's teachings, which were prompted by a sense of the 'inadmissibility' of the labour theory of value and 'the theories of labour wages, ground rent, and capital interest closely associated with it', seemed very suitable for constructing a 'purely' economic distribution theory, which blissfully disregarded social power factors.[5] In this theory, only consumer goods have 'value' because they provide satisfaction to our needs, while the goods of 'higher order' such as labour, land, and capital are considered merely as means to acquire consumer goods. The value of the consumer good they contribute to producing

---

5 Menger, *Grundsätze der Wirtschaftslehre*, II Auflage 1923, S. V

determines their value; the 'isolated agent' assigns a portion of the value of the consumer good to each individual means of production that contributes to its production. If it becomes possible to determine the physical rules of his estimations that distribute and allocate the value of the final product among the various elements of the productive process, then the question of the economic regularity of distribution is resolved. The value shares of labour, land, and capital, expressed in output units of the final product corresponding to their economic significance, would determine the economic value of labour, land, and capital for the isolated economy, and thus also determine wages, interest, and rent as essentially similar economic phenomena of the final value, regardless of social power factors – thereby fulfilling the social purpose of the 'marginal utility'.

This is how the problem of attribution arose, that is the question of the quantitative determinability of the value shares of the individual production factors from the value of the end product, which Menger indicated in his 'Principles' without bringing it to a conclusion. How is this question to be solved now? If the 'pure' economy is to successfully serve its – partly openly admitted, partly denied, but always insistently pursued – purpose of defending the interests of property, then the value and yield calculation must of course state that all factors of production (that is, labour, land, capital) contribute in an essentially identical way to the output of production and that the size of their share in the value of the final product can be determined by the importance of their productive function.[6]

All of this can be easily observed for the isolated economy, and thus the marginalists have also succumbed to the temptation of wanting to construct a modern theory of distribution based on the estimations of the 'isolated agent'. The isolated economy can indeed be understood, following Menger, as a divi-

6 'Indeed, if the existence of the problem is once admitted, one of the most effective arguments of the socialist party is taken away, because as long as it is accepted as true that land and capital have no share in the yield, it must be accepted as true that all income received by land labourers and capitalists is gained at the expense of the workers who created the yield, and as long as this is the case, both forms of income have no other title than that of exploitation. In this respect, defenders of private property have the utmost interest in proving that both land and capital have their share in the yield. The theoretical defence of private ownership of the means of production would hardly have any chance of success if it were true that all yield is exclusively produced by labour and that the problem of yield distribution has been only raised due to the interest of the possessors, while it does not exist in a simple economy'. (Wieser, Theorie der gesellschaftlichen Wirtschaft – Grundriss der Sozialökonomik, 1914, page. 208.) The apologetic character of this 'allocation' is evident in these lines.

sion of certain quantities of labour, land, and raw materials for the production of various consumer goods whose 'importance' leads to corresponding assessments of the elements of production. Indeed, these assessments can be understood, following Wieser and Böhm-Bawerk, as a process of value attribution. However, even the most ingenious motivation for these estimations and attributions does not explain the processes of distribution in the capitalist economy solely based on the 'productive contribution of the factors of production'.

Because all these lines of thought are completely correct, as long as Wieser and Böhm-Bawerk examine the simple economy they themselves constructed, where labour is not separated from ownership, in terms of its economic rationality. The attribution here serves as dedication for productive purposes according to the expected yield, but it is not a basis for distribution. The 'isolated agent', who on a free afternoon nails a few boards together with a hammer to make a table, may equate the value of his free time, the boards, and the hammer (or their 'usefulness') with the value of the table and – using the most complex concepts borrowed from the marginalists – mentally attribute the value of the table to these elements of production based on their 'productive contribution'. Yet, despite this attribution, he remains the exclusive owner of the table, and he can calmly agree to any kind of psychological motivation for his work because his ownership protects him from any negative consequences. He estimates his work and the conditions of his work; he does not remunerate them! However, the marginalists turn this concept of the 'productive contribution', derived from the expedient considerations of a classless planned economy, into a measure of distribution. 'The productive contribution is expressed in absolute figures of the increase in yield to be attributed to the participation of individual factors of production, but it can also be represented as a proportion of the total yield'.[7] Here, attribution becomes a completely different problem! Let us allow both the material and the tools to 'participate', let us include them as equal members in human society along with the marginalists. Then, we must logically realise that each part of the yield depends on the 'participation' of all factors. Are not labour, raw material, and tools equally indispensable? The finest leather will not become a shoe without the 'participation' of the shoemaker, but even the best shoemaker cannot do without the 'participation' of the leather and the last if he wants to produce a pair of shoes. The same applies to every commodity! The realisation of each individual piece and every 'subset' of the end product depends on the 'participation' of each factor, so the entire value of the

7 Wieser, a.a.D, P. page. 212.

commodity would be attributed to the contribution of each individual factor! However, then the production costs would have to be valued at multiple times the production output, which might not disturb the course of the isolated economy in its physically possible existence as an infinitely large value, but for the modern entrepreneur who buys labour and means of production on the market for cash in order to sell the product with a profit, the value of the marginal utility theory would have to approach zero. To escape the compulsion of this response, which arises with compelling consistency from the doctrine's focus on use value, the marginalists resort to the solution of differentiating attribution into 'common' and 'specific'. Experience shows that, although generally only production elements that need to be managed due to their relative scarcity are considered for attribution, some of them can be found in various uses and can be shifted from a 'less important' to a 'more important' use at any time. Their marginal value is always easily discernible from the 'less important' use, which still appears profitable given their relative abundance. In each use, they appear solely with their marginal value and here they constitute a mere cost element. From the value of the end product, only a portion can be attributed to them that corresponds to their cost character, that is, what they can still yield in the less important use. If we then find them as contributing factors in joint use with rare, difficult-to-replace 'specific' production factors that are only suitable for a narrow range of needs – such as mines, factory installations, properties of special quality, gemstones, etc. – then, according to Wieser's formula, the value of the 'common cost goods' must be subtracted from the value of the specific product, and the remaining residual yield is attributed to the contributing specific factor.[8]

Does Wieser really solve the attribution problem in accordance with the conditions he himself sets, i.e., 'completely based on the productive contribution'? The investigation of the physical causality between the contribution of individual production factors and the material magnitude of the yield, which would fix their productive function and thereby provide the measure by which the distribution of the yield takes place, is not even attempted within his solution! The wage, which is the replaceable production factor with a 'lower value' use, is here not derived from the value of the end product as a cost element, but is assumed as a given quantity already in the production and treated as a cost, the deduction of which reveals the value shares of the more or less specific factors.[9] They are merely a difference between the price of labour and the price of the

8 Wieser a.a.D., S. page. 213.

9 Hefendehl. H., *Das Problem der ökonomischen Zurechnung. Eine kritische Untersuchung der Lehre von der funktionellen Verteilung*, Essen, 1922.

end product, which, although it provides a correct description of the capitalist distribution method, does not explain it from the logic of economic action as a whole, as Wieser assumes.

Wieser's attempted solution was even perceived as unsuccessful within the closest circle of the Austrian School.[10] Böhm-Bawerk replaces the 'productive contribution' with the 'share dependent on the contribution to the yield', whose value is supposed to be determined by the replaceability and alternative usability of individual production factors. He starts with the consideration of the unit of production means, which is the entirety of those production resources that are simultaneously employed to produce a specific good or group of goods. Their value is determined by the value of their marginal product, which means the good that, among all the goods for which the unit of production means could have been economically used to produce, has the lowest value.[11] For those production elements that can be replaced by specimens of their kind from other, less valuable uses, the allocation rate is determined by the 'alternative usability', completely independent of their specific complementary use. Their value is always fixed by their substitution value, which is 'the one taken from the loss of utility in those uses from which the replacement specimens are obtained', at a certain magnitude, 'with which they also participate in the distribution of the total value of the productive group to the individual elements'.[12]

This thesis of Böhm-Bawerk, translated from the language of the marginal utility theory into the language of the capitalist market, means that despite the higher profitability of his enterprise, entrepreneur B will not be willing to pay the workers more than they are forced to accept under the pressure of necessity in the inferior enterprise A. This claim certainly agrees with everyday experience within certain limits and is easily understandable as a result of free competition. However, when Böhm-Bawerk attempts to explain the marginal value of labour in case B as its marginal utility in case A, he merely shifts the question instead of answering it. Because even in case A, labour is associated with other production factors in a complementary group, the total value of which is supposed to be derived from the value of their final product ready for consumption. Here too, we still do not know by what method their individual value, that is, their economic share in the total yield of a certain magnitude 'in which they participate in the distribution of the total yield', is fixed. Their individual value in A remains undetermined for us, and it is of little help even if

10 Schumpeter. J. *Bemerkungen über das Zurechnungsproblem*, Zeitschrift für Volkswirtschaft, Sozialpolitik und Verwaltung, 1909. Band 18.

11 Compare Böhm-Bawerk, *Positive Theorie des Kapitals*. IV. Auflage, Jena 1921.

12 Böhm-Bawerk, a.a.D.

we, following Böhm-Bawerk, dissolve the entire group and look for alternative uses for its individual members. The problem of value determination remains just as unresolved in the 'alternative use' as in all the methods of shifting and rearranging with which Böhm-Bawerk operates quite arbitrarily, without considering the technology and the well-known 'law of the minimum' for every farmer, which precisely determines the ratio of motive forces to the mass of raw materials and the individual raw materials to each other and does not allow any addition or withdrawal of a production element without simultaneously enlarging or reducing the overall scope of production. His attempt to separate individual production elements from their given connection in order to test their productivity elsewhere is, theoretically, a completely unacceptable (because practically unthinkable!) process. Any displacement would require a reversion to older or a sudden transition to higher technology!

From the value of the replaceable and alternatively usable production factors, which despite all the considerable effort and ingenuity cannot be determined – that is, from their undetermined substitution value – Böhm-Bawerk ultimately derives the solution to the problem of imputation. If we deduct the substitution quantities from the total yield, then the remainder appears as a share that is attributed to the irreplaceable production factors for their 'contribution to the yield'. With great satisfaction and even greater naivety, Böhm-Bawerk notes that the theoretical distribution formula with which he has described capitalist distribution practice fits 'most accurately' for this practice: the replaceable production means are subtracted by their given substitution value, and the remainder is assigned to the non-'replaceable' elements. The farmer attributes it to 'his land', the mine owner to 'his mine', the manufacturer to 'his factory', and the merchant to 'his entrepreneurial activity'.[13] Yes, certainly, the entrepreneur's profit is calculated, written down, and pocketed in the capitalist economy. But does this process even hint at the quantitative relationship between the 'contribution' and the share in the yield? Clearly, we are dealing with another surplus here, the amount of which remains completely undetermined because the deduction for the 'replaceable production goods' has been left undefined!

The magic trick of distributing the utility of coal to the mine and the miner in such a way that the attributed shares appear to be determined by the size of the physical yield, separately attributing a portion to the contribution of the mine and another portion solely to the miner, has been just as unsuccessful for Böhm- Bawerk as it was for Wieser. However, if we don't know which part

13 Böhm-Bawerk, a.a.D.S.

of the physical yield can be attributed to the individual factors of labour, land, and capital, then the physical 'purely' economic distribution standard is still not found.

Wieser's and Böhm-Bawerk's futile efforts to reinterpret the logic of capitalist economic practice into a logical theory of economics resulted in pseudo-solutions that Schumpeter, their most important student, mercilessly tore up without having to leave their value-theoretical starting point. Schumpeter is secured against their errors by the exact method of his research work, which forces him to describe precisely those external conditions under which the phenomena to be researched are to be uncovered and their functional connections determined. For him, all economic processes are 'exchange relations', which he examines in their purity in an ideal-typical and static economy in which all quantities of goods, all valuations, and all prices are given as fixed data. This means, however, that the same quantities of each good are always demanded and produced and that the quantities of labour and raw materials required for each type of use are necessary in the ratio once established, and are therefore also irreplaceable and immovable. And even if Schumpeter, following the example of Wieser and Böhm-Bawerk, leaves the meaning of the various combinations of usability and replaceability of his assumptions open for him only one type of attribution: in the static economy one or more productive goods belong to each consumption good, which cannot be replaced and cannot be used 'otherwise', i.e. are irreplaceable and indispensable at the given point. Schumpeter does not shy away from the most extreme conclusions that result from his theoretical assumptions: he calculates for each individual production good all value functions that result from the actual use of its individual subsets, i.e. the entire value of the consumption good in whose production it participated has to. 'This is the great crux of the theory of distribution: workers, capitalists and landowners, all of them or at least the productive goods they own are irreplaceable in any production. It is easy to show that productive success depends on all three categories and that there is no criterion for distinguishing one factor of production over the other in this respect'.

From Wieser's and Böhm-Bawerk's futile efforts to reinterpret the logic of capitalist economic practice into a logical economic theory, pseudo-solutions emerged, which their most significant student, Schumpeter, mercilessly tore apart without having to abandon their value-theoretical starting point.[14] He is safeguarded against their errors by the exact method of his research work,

14 Schumpeter J., *Das Wesen und der Hauptinhalt der theoretischen Rationlaökonomie.* Leipzig. (Dunker und Humblot) 1908.

which compels him to precisely describe those external conditions under which the phenomena to be researched are to be uncovered and their functional connections determined. For him, all economic processes are 'exchange relations', which he examines in their purity in an ideal-typical, static economy where all quantities of goods, valuations, and prices are given as fixed data. This implies that the same quantities of each good are always demanded and produced, and the quantities of labour and raw materials required for each use are necessary in the once-established ratio, thus also being irreplaceable and immovable.

The answer that Schumpeter provides, starting from the use value, is certainly correct, although one could answer with the same degree of correctness that the use value of the working conditions and tools is nothing without the purposefully used labour, and likewise, labour is nothing without the conditions of production! Both answers are equally right or wrong, but neither of them allows for economic determinants to be derived for capitalist distribution. The separation of the worker from the means of production clearly rebels against a theory that seeks to transfer the valuations of the isolated economy, meaning an economy controlled by purposive will and guided so that the maximum possible use values are obtained with a minimum of sacrifices under given conditions, to any externally regulated economic order with 'labour' without ownership and 'income' without labour. Value attribution has failed, and with it, the role of marginal utility as an economic theory that derives economic phenomena not from the specific social structure of each economy but from a constantly unchanging internal logic of every economy, has been played out. The mitigating circumstance of a 'principle possibility' of the as-yet-unfound solution, for which Schumpeter argues, should not preserve the appearance of viability. But what does he want to base it on? Let's listen:

This moment is certainly solvable. Any doubt is excluded by the fact that values and prices of productive goods are in no way different from those of consumer goods, especially as they are handled with the same certainty by practical economic agents and are equally fixed at any given time. Thus, practice has solved the problem and thereby proves its solvability through action.[15]

Schumpeter's exact logic makes a peculiar leap here! Indeed, capitalist practice solves the distribution problem through action, by forming wages, rent, and entrepreneurial profit. However, can we be certain that within these historical categories of a class-differentiated society, they can be understood or

15 Schumpeter, a.a.D., P. 258.

causally integrated into the economic process using the concepts of 'subjective' or 'pure' economics, which fundamentally negate the historical specificity of modern income types?

Capitalist practice is faced here with a doctrine that, for half a century, has been trying to solve the main problems of modern society like a puzzle with various solutions but only manages to prove one thing: it cannot explain capitalist practice without abandoning itself. To quantitatively determine income types derived from labour, i.e., from a productive function, and all other income types flowing from the ownership title, they must first be qualitatively distinguished, i.e., differentiated in their essential characteristics. However, this means recognising and admitting that their level is not determined by economic factors but by social factors, not by 'productive contributions' but by class power, not by 'performance' but by influence. The bourgeois science of economics cannot not exceed the limits of this knowledge.

The practical solvability of the distribution problem through capitalist action, therefore, signifies its theoretical insolvability through the means of marginal value theory, which disguises ownership as utility and achievement, and labour as a commodity, aiming to obscure the parasitism of landowners and the creative personality of workers. The marginal utility of this doctrine, to which it owes its fame and its official position, is conditioned by its 'participation' in the cover-up of social contradictions and by its 'productive contribution' to the defense of the property which it is willed to deliver, even if so it makes an agreement on 'the theory' and on the nature of its main problems and their overall context increasingly difficult. The bourgeoisie can see it as proven with satisfaction that wages are always equal to the income, that is, 'attributable' to the worker and that on top of that 'wage payment is one of the brakes on production, while entrepreneurial profit is not (Schumpeter, 1934)'. The tragicomedy of economic 'value attribution' becomes quite understandable when we recall Marx's words:

... the class struggle ... sounded the death knell of scientific bourgeois economics. It was no longer a question of whether this or that theorem was true, but whether it was useful or harmful, convenient or inconvenient for capital, whether it was in accordance with the police or not. Altruistic research was replaced by polemics, and unbiased scientific investigation was replaced by the guilty conscience and bad intentions of apologetics.[16]

16 Marx, Das Kapital, Volume 1. From the preface to the second edition.

CHAPTER 11

Wealth Levy and Socialisation, *Der Kampf* (1919), Vol. 7: 291–4

The wealth of private enterprises consists of consumer goods, means of production, gold and silver coins, and claims against private individuals and the state. The war, which lasted four years and was marked by the criminal waste of human lives and resources, consumed an enormous portion of tangible assets. However, the powerful of yesterday managed, through the refined techniques of modern life, to cloak the devastation of war in a form of wealth. Everything that the state extracted from the economy for the unproductive purposes of war was paid for in the most generous manner. The printing press worked tirelessly, and to make the economy receptive to ever-increasing amounts of paper money a part of the notes thrown into circulation was repeatedly withdrawn through the issuance of war bonds. And now the game could begin anew; now the state could entice the war industry to new activity with the lure of high prices, rallying the broadest layers of war beneficiaries (the suppliers and chain dealers) to a new spirit of endurance patriotism – offering them all new war bonds at the onset of the fatigue that must inevitably follow from the oversaturation with paper money.

For four years, predatory exploitation took place in both industry and agriculture. The farmer had his cattle and seed corn taken away from him, while the entrepreneur's operation was 'converted' for war purposes and exploited until all machines and equipment were completely worn out – items that were difficult to replace during the war. New acquisitions were impossible in both the countryside and the city: the war consumed all supplies and all labour. But what does it matter? Even if there were no investment opportunities, and machines and equipment were not renewed, houses were not repaired, and fields were not fertilised, the economy turned into a heap of rubble – yet there was even more paper money in the hands of individuals, and the success of the new war bonds (the seventh and eighth) could again serve as a fine testimony to the determination of the population to endure.

While the tangible assets of the economy shrank due to consumption and wear, while the shortage of raw materials and resources cut off every possibility for productive work, state debt and the annual interest requirement grew ever more powerful. The criminal carelessness of yesterday's rulers and their followers promised private individuals an income from interest through war bonds – thus providing them with a claim to a portion of the annual product of the economy, which had now reached a dizzying height and is expected to be honoured at a time when both the power of the old command structure and (unfortunately) the productive work of society have been broken.

And now, since the people have freed themselves from the rulers who imposed the tribute upon them, they will also rid themselves of that tribute. The income from income title should disappear; the holder of war bonds should lose the right to effortlessly benefit from the meagre returns of the economy. The call for socialisation – that is, for the transfer of the means of production into the hands of society – is joined by the demands for immediate wealth taxation, the abolition of the rentier system, and the eradication of the right to the products of others' labour.

The first goal to be achieved through wealth taxation in our case would be to cleanse the economy of war bonds, transferring them into the hands of the state. War bonds represent the portion of private wealth that has already been withdrawn from productive purposes and is intended merely for the acquisition of an income title. Their removal can occur without upheaval and without further diminishing the productive basis of the economy. They are, economically speaking, an idle part of an individual's wealth; their taxation would reduce income without constraining work and earning opportunities. Thus, the wealth tax would primarily be paid by the entire trading and industrial world, especially through war bonds – and even more so, as their acceptance at full nominal value, despite their low market price, would have to be considered a gain by the holders of war bonds. For a short time, war bonds would even become a highly sought-after paper for the payment of the wealth tax, which on one hand would enable small savers, exempt from the wealth tax, to sell their war bonds favourably, and on the other hand would guarantee a strong return of war bonds to the state treasury.

The wealth tax aims to abolish, if not immediately, then gradually, the larger idle fortunes. It must temporarily halt before the smaller fortunes, which essentially form a household reserve fund and have been accumulated through personal labour and restraint, as well as before productive assets. The relationship between fixed and circulating capital is fairly well established through technical development; a sudden withdrawal of a larger sum of money from a business that would force the entrepreneur to reduce the number of employed workers and the raw materials to be processed would not only diminish social goods production but would also significantly reduce the profitability of the enterprise. Here, a wealth tax is not appropriate; rather, a corresponding income tax is in order.

Socialisation transfers individual industries or sectors recognised by society as 'ripe' into the possession of society. It attaches itself to the means of production and strips them of their function as capital by gradually abolishing the propertyless wage labourer. One can also easily imagine a kind of division of labour between socialisation actions and wealth tax. While socialisation pertains to the means of production, the wealth tax targets money capital in all its forms – thus all the various claims to products of others' labour from the legal title of ownership.

Socialisation combats the capitalist entrepreneur, while the wealth tax targets the idle rentier. The productively invested capital should not be diminished by the wealth tax – and yet, the wealth tax cannot stop before it. The capital of the idle rentier is not always 'idle' itself; it is not solely invested in war bonds, even though the idling of industry has led to such a significant success of war bonds, meaning a large part of the monetary capital has been transformed into war bonds. Modern credit, which has called the rentier to life as a specific social phenomenon, seizes all the idle funds and makes them available to industry, where they can enable the carefree existence of those who own nothing but stocks. The capital of corporations and other large industrial enterprises partly comprises the capital of disemployed beneficiaries, which flows to industry through banks and is managed by skilled personnel, including technical and commercial staff. Part of it is the property of the idle rentier, which can also be entirely confiscated by the state, and yet it is still productively invested capital that cannot be withdrawn from the sphere of production without harming the economy.

This apparent contradiction is easily resolved when the state, through a wealth tax, seizes ownership titles and itself steps into the rights of the taxpayer as a creditor. The normal course of production is neither disturbed nor affected by this process; the creditor stands outside the business. However, this paves and facilitates the way for socialisation. With a strong capture of the largest fortunes, the state thus becomes the owner of stocks and other large enterprises, which, in the event of expropriation, have already been partially expropriated through the wealth tax as compensation. Consequently, the total amount needed to completely compensate the previous owners would be smaller and would be covered by the funds that flow to the state through the wealth tax.

In some cases, the wealth tax will only serve as preliminary work for socialisation – while, conversely, socialisation always prepares the way for the wealth tax. The significant role that credit plays in modern industrial life makes the transfer of production means from private to social ownership such a complicated task. Banks subject all liquid financial resources of society to the control of financial magnates. A mere confiscation of enterprises, their uncompensated expropriation, would not only affect the capitalist entrepreneur but also all those whose money has flowed to their enterprise through banks: insurance companies, health funds, trade unions, and charitable institutions would be driven to stop payments, and many of the workers' and small employees' emergency funds would be lost. The fear of uncompensated expropriation would paralyse many industries that cannot currently proceed to socialisation, leading to many substantial reasons for ensuring compensation for entrepreneurs expropriated through the socialisation of their enterprises. However, expropriation with compensation strips the capitalist of his social function as a production manager while revealing his exploitative role in appropriating others' labour, making him a rentier without disguise. Through expropriation with compensation, he becomes the idle rentier, the best-suited subject of the wealth tax. Since there is no place for him in the community of labour, the wealth tax must follow socialisation and, although slowly, must inevitably deal with the idle.

The close relationship between socialisation and the wealth tax arises naturally from the dual character of the capitalist entrepreneur as both a production manager and an owner of surplus value. In the transition to a common economy, both his social and economic functions are stripped away from him. Socialisation takes care of the former, while the wealth tax addresses the latter. This deprivation does not necessarily have to coincide completely in time. The interplay between socialisation and the wealth tax is both a question of practicality and a matter of power. Both actions can follow one another quite quickly, for example, if the proletariat seizes power, but under certain political conditions, they can extend over a long period, and both must be fully realised before socialism can take root.

The war has devastated and consumed the national wealth and, in its place, handed over private claims on the yield of labour in the coming years. The wealth tax, no matter how high it may be set, is therefore unable to put the state in possession of assets that could be used for purchasing food, undertaking emergency work, or improving wages and salaries. The wealth that can be taxed consists only of paper claims, which are now to be settled in an orderly manner through taxation so that they do not have to be eliminated in general confusion and despair through a state bankruptcy. This wealth tax, which can only extinguish claims on the future yield of the economy, will not change anything for the income of the working classes in the meantime and will not mean any increase in goods for them. And yet its significance extends far beyond the immediate benefit of annual interest savings, which currently corresponds to merely a saving in banknote issuance. It is a protest of the people against the legacy of the hated war, against the power of the overthrown and expelled, who, through the tribute they have imposed on the nation, continue to demand their existence; it is a protest against the rule of capital. It does not enrich, but it liberates, and for that reason, it has become a necessity for us.

CHAPTER 12

The Harmony of Interests, the 'Common Man', and a Better Gentleman, *Arbeit und Wirtschaft*, 1923: 589–92

If someone believes that satisfying their particular personal tastes outweighs the additional costs compared to satisfying those needs with uniform products, then one cannot objectively prove them wrong ... If my friend prefers to dress, live, and eat according to his own preferences and not do what everyone else does, then he cannot be reproached for it ... If he wants to furnish his home according to his own personal taste and not according to that of the furniture manufacturer, he cannot be disproven with reasons ...

The understanding that Dr. [Ludwig] Mises shows in his hefty book '*Die Gemeinwirtschaft*' toward his friend's individual preferences suggests that he would also refrain from criticising the friend's wife, who likely enjoys wrapping herself in luxurious furs and flowing silks held together by jewels. After all, happiness 'lies precisely in the satisfaction of one's desires', and Mr. Mises, as a proponent of pleasure ethics, is concerned with his friends' happiness. He believes that the capitalist economy, in which his friend can furnish his home and table to his liking, is the best and the only viable economic order.

Whoever can afford it should enjoy, says the liberal Mr. Mises. And in order to ensure that the cheerful enjoyment of the wealthy is no longer disturbed by the unpleasant miasma of doubt about the moral legitimacy of their elevated lifestyle – a doubt that creeps into the offices of capital magnates and the boudoirs of their wives from the socialist-tinged, poisoned atmosphere of public life – he now seeks to prove that socialism is an entirely irrational economic system! While one may no longer find the fundamental opposition to socialism, or the boldness to openly and freely champion private ownership of the means of production, Mr. Mises offers just that, along with the necessary philosophical and economic 'perspectives'. He now calls socialism to the battleground, and the fight shall be waged with the 'weapons of the mind'.

The mind first manifests itself like that of a Homeric hero. The opponent is greeted with insults. Socialism, he claims, is nothing more than 'the rationalisation of petty resentments', a doctrine that 'glorifies the raging instincts of envy and revenge as a world-historical mission' and draws its conclusions 'from the muddled thoughts of an absurd system'. The opponent is to be intimidated with threats. 'All efforts to realise socialism lead only to the destruction of society ...

The population of industrial areas will either die out or emigrate ... Once again, nomadic tribes from the steppes of the East could gallop across Europe, plundering as they go – who could resist them in a sparsely populated land when the weapons inherited from the advanced technology of capitalism have worn out?' (Page 498).

However, for those who are less terrified by the defencelessness of a sparsely populated Europe and the nomads on swift horses than by capitalism, who cannot suppress their instincts of envy and revenge even in the face of such dangers, the dreadful name of Malthus is invoked. In vain does one try to soothe their conscience with the observation that with rising culture and increasing prosperity, population growth tends to slow down. For Mises, however, mercilessly counters that this only holds true under private ownership, and that 'every reason to refrain from procreation disappears the moment family formation can occur without economic sacrifice, because the support of children falls to society'. (Page 187) Thus, the socialist future harbours within it two equally disastrous possibilities: overpopulation with legal interventions in reproductive freedom or the desolation of once-flourishing cultural centres. Let everyone choose what seems worse to them! But it doesn't have to come to that. According to Mises, society is a product of will and action, and it forges its own future. Society approaches socialism because the vast majority wants it, because the vast majority views socialism as a system that generates greater prosperity. And 'if there is a change in this perception, then socialism is doomed'.

In order to bring about this change – an endeavour that many lecturers famously take on every year – Mises critically examines the economic structure of all conceivable socialist and pseudo-socialist systems and always finds them incompatible with rational economic management. There is no cost accounting, no standard of distribution! Instead of the marvellous system in which the capitalist 'calculates' meagre wages for the worker, for the 'performance of the machines' (machines whose design is usually foreign to him), and for the 'performance of the land' (which he wouldn't even know how to weed), that is, for the 'productive contributions of the material factors' invented by marginal utility theorists, socialism would institute a 'method of distribution that grants no owner or entrepreneur a fundamentally different position than other members of society'. In fact, the 'shares' allotted to the machine and the land could not even be determined! However, for any properly functioning bourgeois, the 'fundamentally different position of owners and entrepreneurs' – the friend, for example, with his home and table set according to his own taste – forms part of the worldview, and thus the calculation of profits is seen as the only meaningful purpose of economic activity. For him, an economy oriented toward meeting needs is incomprehensible. And, quite logically, Mises sees socialism as nothing but 'the senseless behaviour of a mindless apparatus'. (Page 107). For those who equate profit with reason, profitlessness is, naturally, irrational!

As a true man of science, Mises is always accompanied by economic theory during his journey through the ill-fated realms of socialism. When he rejects socialist distribution and sees in capitalism the guarantee that every merit will receive its due reward, he does not do so arbitrarily, but in the name of the theory he represents. The bourgeois representatives of economics may disagree on the determining factors of capitalist distribution; yet, despite the diversity of their opinions and the roundabout ways in which they arrive at their solutions to the 'problem of attribution', there is always one point of agreement in their complex arguments. No matter how the capitalist calculates the wages of the worker and the interest for himself – whether according to Böhm-Bawerk, Schumpeter, Clark, or Wieser – he always arrives at the correct amount. Exactly what he pays out, and exactly what he pockets, corresponds to the performance of the worker, the machine, and the land, for which he, as an authorised representative, submits the bill. Mises, whose scientific rigor no socialist distribution system can withstand, is content with the unfinished state of bourgeois theories of attribution. The results of these theories suffice for him to affirm the superiority of capitalist distribution. This system is unsurpassable, the only possible one. Here, the 'natural wage' is set at such a level that the worker receives the full yield of his labour, that is, everything attributed to labour comes to him. And if this 'natural wage' – everything the capitalist allocates to labour – does not allow the worker to dress, live, and eat as he pleases, if it is not enough to satisfy the special wishes of personal taste or even to purchase uniform mass-produced goods in sufficient quantity, this is simply the nature of this natural wage. The happiness that lies in the fulfillment of one's desires is an ethical principle only for friends. For the worker who has 'his own desires', Mises tries to objectively prove that he is in the wrong. The limits of the 'natural wage' must not be surpassed no matter how tightly they are drawn to satisfy one's pleasures. Only malicious envy could want to break these limits, and it is only from the sad fact 'that even today the common man tends to view the state as a source of rent from which he wants to draw as much income as possible' (Page 61), and that he 'dislikes unearned income, as long as someone else and not he himself is receiving it' (Page 257), that Mr. Mises can explain the dissatisfaction of the common man with the status quo.

Socialism is not only a vision of a bleak future; by attempting to disrupt economic forces through constraints, it already becomes a cause of impoverishment. Capitalism is tied to the full freedom of economic activity, to free competition. Through free competition, capitalism develops productive forces; through competition, it creates the wealth of markets; through competition, it places every man in the right position. With the removal of guild barriers, 'anyone' can become wealthy if they participate in the general competition. But 'despite all these experiences and facts, the worker seeks his salvation in uniting with other workers'. (Page 401)

The Marxist doctrine of the unity of interests among all proletarians is to blame for the fact that the worker, instead of following the capitalist principle by underbidding his fellow workers to find buyers and increasing his sales by extending the workday – in other words, following the path that makes the rich richer – chooses the restrictions of the union over the freedom of competition! By not thinking of the harmony of interests, which liberal social theory speaks of, but instead focusing on his own class position, he disrupts this harmony and thus his own happiness. Mises has no doubt that the worker 'has only been turned away from liberalism by the incitement of his basest instincts'. And that wasn't even difficult, 'because awakening the evil in man is always rewarding'. Mises readily admits that even in capitalist circles, there is much sinning against the liberal principle of competition, but while he sees only evil in the unions of the 'common man', he views the associations of the elite as often a tool of historical reason. For example, the price-raising policies of cartels can only remain effective over long periods of time when there is monopolistic control of natural resources, and in such cases, through increased prices, they enforce the careful use of non-renewable goods, like coal and iron.

The poor woman in childbirth and the disabled worker now shiver in their unheated rooms to stretch the coal supply over the few thousand years for which it is secured, while the rich man enjoys the comfort of warmth. Smart management, and yet – what joyful pleasure! Is capitalism not the best, the 'only possible' economic system? Should perhaps Mr. Mises's friend, with his home furnished to personal taste, be put on a meagre coal ration? No! That would be a state interference in private life. And after all, since he is not a common man but a superior one, it is his function to save on the enjoyment of others' lives, not on his own. That is the rationality of the capitalist system: capital accumulation does not diminish enjoyment. Some go without, while others create new capital, all without sacrifice. But a socialist accumulation, as a consciously desired expansion of society's productive base, appears highly dubious to the professor.

So Mr. Mises fights with intellectual weapons for private property, interest, and profit. And the bourgeois men of theory, especially those of practice, show the greatest appreciation for this intellectualism and these weapons. Finally, a man and a work! He sees in the unions the workings of 'evil' and in social insurance a 'harmful influence on social morality'. That is science! This mutual admiration should not be disturbed by disparaging criticism. Whoever praises Mr. Mises surely deserves his praise. This 'standard work' and its enthusiastic critics form a harmony of interests that even the 'common man' can understand. And it's not even difficult!

CHAPTER 13

Mr. Ottmar Spann's 'Tablecloth Set Yourself' (1922), Vol. 6: 178–82

In Max Adler's 'Causality and Teleology in the Dispute about Science'[1] we find a reference to the peculiar mode of appearance of natural law in the social field. The fact that here 'all regularity always acts only within a specific functional context, which is sustained by the relationship of people to one another as practical, that is, purposeful beings, continually brings teleological aspects into critical research in the social sphere'. Now, Ottmar Spann, in his 'Foundations of Economics',[2] attempts to make purposefulness a fundamental concept of economics without being deterred by the question of whether a society lacking any unified, purposeful regulation of its economic existence can be grasped through teleological means.

He sets out eagerly and joyfully to rescue economics from the crude conception and conceptual form of a causal science and to establish it as a science of an entirely different nature, 'namely as a pure science of purpose', on the ruins of individualism, which in economics only saw the 'mechanical' aspects – the 'quantities of goods', the 'quantitative relationships', the 'attraction and repulsion of materials', which are 'indeed purely causal, that is, conceptually causal in a similar way to physics and mechanics or in the mechanistic psychology of association masses'. As an example of a mechanistic-quantitative view of the economy, as a simple sum of commodities, Marx is now quoted, with the well-known words at the beginning of his 'Capital': 'The wealth of societies in which the capitalist mode of production prevails appears as an immense collection of commodities, the individual commodity as its elementary form'. And now, ridicule and scorn follow: 'This mechanical concept of the economy, which still secretly dominates all teaching images, seems to me like the old folk riddle: What are the twelve apostles doing in heaven? A dozen! Instead of saying what they are doing, they are simply counted together!' (Page 78.)

So says Spann – Marx, however, determines the appearance, the form of bourgeois wealth in the introductory words, in order to draw the analysis of this

1 Marx Studien, I Band. Wien 1904. S. 421.

2 Jena, 1921. 2 Auflage.

form into the focus of the following theoretical consideration. But that was no less of a gain, when the problem of theoretical national economy was formulated comprehensively and exhaustively for the first time.

With this, not less was achieved than the problem of theoretical political economy being completely and exhaustively formulated for the first time.[3] While for Ricardo, for whom bourgeois society represented an eternal and natural form of human existence, value was a natural attribute of goods as products of human labour, Marx examines the historically determined conditions that confer commodity character on the products of labour. 'As the creator of use-values, as useful labour, labour is an existence condition of humans independent of all social formations. Only in a society where use-values are products of independently conducted private labours exchanged as private property, that is, in bourgeois society, do the products of labour become commodities as far as they are also use-values'. In the commodity form of products, the societal character of individuals as independent producers of commodities comes to expression. They work independently of each other but, for whatever reasons, for one another, and thus their individual labour is only a part of the social total labour, which appears as a unity in the market through the exchange process.

'The mysterious aspect of the commodity form simply consists in the fact that it reflects back to individuals the societal characters of their own labour as objective characters of the products of labour themselves, as societal natural attributes of these things. Therefore, the societal relationship of producers to the totality appears as a social relationship of objects existing independently of them.[4]' By determining the form in which bourgeois wealth appears at 'first glance', Marx thus arrives at the revelation of the 'fetish character' of the commodity – but, of course, only after the long and laborious path of a historically conceptual analysis. Spann, fully occupied with placing the inscription 'mechanistic-quantitative view of the economy as a simple sum of commodities' on the spoil of the first introductory sentence, finds no time to read further in the 'Capital' and exclaims triumphantly: 'What are the twelve apostles doing in heaven? A dozen!' Indeed, if one wishes to know what they are doing there, it is not enough to eavesdrop at the keyhole; one must be able to force one's way inside as well!

The remaining objections of Spann against the 'individualities' Smith, Ricardo, and Marx, who allegedly overlooked the entirety in economics, are so

3 Hilferding: Zur Problemstellung der theoretischen Nationalökonomie. "Neue Zeit". Jahrgang XXIII. S. 104.

4 Marx: Kapital. Band I. S. 36. Volksausgabe.

grotesque that their emergence appears possible only through the assumption of a consistent reluctance to read further. There has never been an individualism in economics that only saw punctual mechanics, overlooking the significance of productive forces, and least of all among the classical economists, whose advocacy of free trade seemed to be a support for the productive forces within the global economic framework, or even in the case of Marx, who recognised the development of productive forces as the decisive driving force of social events. Such a contradiction in research methods, between individualism and universalism, does not exist in reality, and Spann's classification principle of social sciences, which was led astray by blind trust in the romantic reactionary Adam Müller (referring to Adam Müller von Nitterdorf), is entirely unfounded.[5]

By critically dealing with 'individualism and mechanism', Spann now seeks to clear the path for a 'universalistic' economics in the spirit of Adam Müller. 'That which Marx and others, who were supposed to construct a universalistic theoretical structure, found difficult, Adam Müller succeeded in: to trace the concept of wholeness in the individual appearance, lively and concrete, everywhere'. Spann now declares that it is up to him to take up this legacy and to guide economics towards the recognition of the organic connections 'linking the economy with the entirety of society and history' through his methodological investigations. However, Spann's methodology takes its starting point from a timeless and spaceless concept of the economy, disregarding the 'spirit that points towards history and sociology'. For him, the economy is the 'weighing of means for ends', and the world is the 'causality that derives its justification only from those 'values', ends it serves'. The 'values', 'ends' are ultimate purposes that already have their own justification, such as the preservation of life, higher spiritual content, such as science, art, and religion.

The purposes on the one hand, and their realisation in material and spiritual existence on the other hand, are 'completely different things', separating like 'fire and water', and everything that is an objective has a different position and role in human society than the economy, where purposes are 'leading', and the economy is merely 'servile'. The purpose of the economy, according to Spann, is placed in a different value level than the economy itself; however, their opposition is soon dissolved by the ambiguity of the concept of 'purpose' encountered in Spann's work. Here, purpose or goal is at once the practically valid will that sets a series of means in motion, thus the ideal that is realised

5 Compare. E. Schmidt. S. 51.

in the material realm through external causality. At the same time, it is also what exists independently of the means, the moral norm, or in another case, the 'final link in a series of means'. Whether he claims that 'the economy itself is not a goal and cannot become a goal in any way' (page 36), or that 'the attainment of goals constitutes the content of the economy', 'goal and economy are as distinct as fire and water', 'the economy is based on goal attainment', one can, at best, amidst all the confusion, come to the one conclusion, which Spann also intended, that the economy, as a means related to economic goals, is a means to an end – which no one will dispute!

However, what may appear to be a harmless play with words and concepts is indeed a 'method'. From the subserviency of the economy, Spann deduces the subserviency of all goods-creating work, which now becomes a 'conditionally passive' and 'passive good', equated with all other 'performing' goods. 'Only to the extent that work is done for the sake of joy, the activation of one's abilities, and for the sake of moral value, such as the work of statesmen, politicians, actors, critics, journalists, scholarly researchers, artists, priests, purely for their own sake', is considered by Spann as an end in itself, no longer a means, or in the worst case, a means of a nobler origin. From this hierarchy of labour, as Spann believes, necessarily arises a hierarchically structured society, in which 'self-sufficient' work, 'the work of a nobler origin', naturally forms a pinnacle. The philosophical playfulness of the 'foundations' becomes, in the 'True State', a weapon against democracy![6]

The philosophically adorned self-evidence that the economy is a means to an end may be sufficient in the realm of 'rooted structures', of 'performance-related interconnected actions' and goods that serve the same ultimate purpose, such as in closed domestic economies or in Robinsonades, to comprehend economic processes that contain no social or economic problems in their clarity, as obvious as Spann's discoveries are. However, the economy becomes an economic problem, a potential subject of economic-theoretical research, only in the commodity-producing society where the social cohesion of individual labours is torn apart by private property, and the social relations of people, insofar as they are of an economic nature, only come to expression through exchange. Exchange becomes the central economic phenomenon here, and the problems of the market become problems of the society producing for the market. What ensures the continuous flow of goods to the market? Where do the flood and ebb of commodities come from? What determines their adaptation in terms of type and category to needs, and what dictates their

6 Ottmar Spann: Der wahre Staat.

distribution among individual societal groups and individuals? What replaces the purposeful will in the subordination of all individual labours to the overall needs of society? The task is to discover the law of motion of the market, which in a society working for the market must also become a general law of social movement. By demonstrating that the seemingly objective relations of commodities are actually human relations among commodity producers, Marx causally traced the colorful confusion of seemingly arbitrary market processes back to the nature of human relationships under which the necessary work for the preservation of society is expended, that is, the necessary quantity of commodities is produced. We find the totality of these relations, the social being of people, reflected in market processes. As labour value is not a 'natural' product of labour but a product of specific labour relations, exchange value is also a product of the particular role that individual commodity owners hold within the labour process. It is neither 'mechanistic' nor 'objective', as Spann claims, but a social phenomenon that can be *historically* explained within the framework of Marxism. The price of the commodity labour power is determined by the proletarian's lack of ownership, while the price of all other commodities is influenced by the 'more' or 'less' of capital ownership that has become necessary due to technological development in order to control the production elements of the given branch of labour. The distribution thus appears to be causally grounded, that is, explained by the course of the capitalist production and reproduction process.

What can the Spannian conceptualisation of 'economy as the weighing of means to ends', 'economy as the realm of means', contribute to understanding the phenomena in the commodity-producing society? 'When A buys from B, they only serve each other through the exchange of their goods, but the resulting complex structure as such does not serve anyone; as such, it has no set purposes'. (Page 137.) Now the actual problem of political economy arises – securing goods for the constantly renewing total needs of a society lacking a consciously intended regulation of overall labour. The structure of exchange, which 'formally consists only of the interlocking of two performances', does not 'serve anyone' and is not a realm of ultimate purpose values. From the given assumptions, Spann correctly deduces that 'only the buyer is a self-determining party in the exchange', who essentially 'has an estimation of zero for their goods', 'virtually integrating themselves into the exchange structure established by the buyers'. (Page 141.) Stinnes follows as Friday the command of Robinson – the complex structure leads back to the 'one-rooted' Robinsonade. Spann's excursion into the field of political economy thus ends as a 'self-purpose', meaning it does not serve the purposes of economic knowledge. With this, according to Spann, he reveals himself as a means of 'nobler stock' and secures his creator the right to engage in goods-producing labour, from which the Professor himself benefits, chopping it down from above!

Spann assures us several times on every page that society is a primary entity, a totality, yet he only presents individuals who bind each other as bearers of purposeful ideas and take into account the self-willed binding, essentially just the same arrangement of 'atoms' that he supposedly condemns so much. If the bearers of purposeful ideas are to be conceived as connected, then they must already be conceptually understood as socially oriented towards connecting will, as socially associated individuals in Marx's sense.[7] The life of society with its social, that is, intellectual and physical means can only be conceptually understood when the creative efforts of the individual human, in whom and through whom society lives, are recognised as social. The labour theory of value reveals to us the regularity of social events because, in Marxist terms, 'the social is already given as a precondition of the individual'. Spann's 'universalistic' conceptualisation – 'the use of the railway facilitates transportation, the use of land provides food, economy as the aggregate of productive means' – does not encompass social creation but rather individual fulfillment of needs, thus conjuring an iron ring around the individual, preventing them from finding their way to society.

Finally, after many unsuccessful attempts to create space for the value increase, this one aspect of the 'real economy' which seems to have no place in the 'valid context of purposes', Spann resigns and leaves it to the individualist concept of exchange of the 'pure theory' of individualistic marginal utility doctrine. As Adam Müller has already shown, the 'ignoring and elimination of the concept of exchange' does not result in any loss but rather a gain for the economy. And Spann can do so with confidence! He aptly sums up the outcome of his logical-methodological investigations in the following words: The economy resembles the 'Tablecloth that Sets Itself', accompanying people through life and serving their spiritual contents and goals, either well or poorly. And as for the bill? Well, apparently, that's what the twelve apostles in heaven may argue about!

7 Max Adler: "Zur Erkenntniskritik der Sozialwissenschaften in Marxistische Probleme". Stuttgart 1919.

CHAPTER 14

Imperialism: *Der Kampf* (1927), Vol. 1: 7–12

Is modern imperialism, as the advance of highly developed industrial states into areas with pre-capitalist economies – itself a necessary consequence of the capitalist mode of production and appropriation – ultimately only be able to assert its existence through bloody wars for colonial markets and in ever-expanding political catastrophes?

This question, which Rosa Luxemburg[1] already posed and affirmed, is raised once again by Fritz Sternberg,[2] undeterred and unswayed by criticism of Rosa's book, in order to examine and affirm it along the same lines of thought. He describes Luxemburg's work, which he refers to as 'epoch-making', while simultaneously treating it as a still flawed draft of his own work, which uncovers facts completely in 'all contexts and consequences' that have hitherto been partially known and correctly perceived.

Imperialism is necessary for capitalism in a certain phase; it is a logical necessity. Behind imperialism, behind the intrusion into non-capitalist states, the state must position itself (Page 266). In this 'certain phase', individual-state capitalism comes into play when, within its own borders, its 'non-capitalist space' – consisting of agriculture and craftsmanship – has been destroyed and absorbed by the expansion of capitalist rule, or has already been significantly restricted in scope. With its disappearance, the possibility of complete and full realisation of profit within national boundaries vanishes for the capitalist entrepreneur and the economic pressure of permanent crisis, which would now have to set in, is averted by advancing into colonial lands. For Rosa Luxemburg, the existence of third parties remained a necessary precondition for the possibility of capital accumulation itself, without which capitalism, whose purpose is to constantly expand the foundation of its dominion – and thus, to create new capital – rather than squander and waste the spoils, would lose its entire substance. However, the consumption of workers is already predetermined and limited by the size of the variable portion of capital; the free professions – officials, clergy, artists – have no independent source of purchasing power and are already encompassed economically in the consumption of

1 Rosa Luxemburg: "Accumulation of Capital", Berlin 1918.
2 Fritz Sternberg: "Imperialism", Malik Verlag, Berlin.

the two major classes: capitalists and workers. The capitalists save in order to accumulate – so who can be the buyer, the consumer of the societal portion of goods that is supposed to enable accumulation in the first place? 'This much is clear', says Rosa Luxemburg, 'neither workers nor capitalists can be this'.[3] Their consumption is only possible if there are buyers beyond the capitalist classes with their own purchasing power – 'third parties' – who continually absorb the surplus of saving capital. If they are not nearby, they must be found afar. And if they don't do it willingly, they will be forcibly compelled!

We find the very same explanation of the economic root of imperialism, stemming from the laws of capital accumulation, in Sternberg as well, in whose voluminous book only the sometimes less fortunate terminology is a product of the author himself. Sternberg also recognises, despite his entanglement in Rosa's thoughts, that accumulation does not require the presence of these 'third parties' who inject their money into the capitalist cycle with each turn, and that it can and does take place when the mass of surplus value emerges in the material form of means of production and consumer goods and is supplied by capitalists in this material form as constant and variable capital of production. He seeks to rescue her critique of Marx's schemes of expanded reproduction and all its implications through mathematical proof, demonstrating that the accumulation of capital, which enlarges the productive apparatus, must subsequently bring about an increase in the value measures of the finished products, which can no longer be completely absorbed within the 'capitalist nexus', that is, they cannot be bought either by the workers or by the accumulating capitalists. Within the 'capitalist space', productive capacity is constantly greater than consumer capacity, which means that the supply of consumer goods exceeds its market possibilities, and the 'unabsorbable residue of consumption' must be sold in a 'pre-capitalist economic circle' under constant risk of crisis. As a country becomes increasingly capitalist, its non-capitalist space within its own borders diminishes more and more, and the necessity grows to exploit a foreign territory with a pre-capitalist economy as a market for the 'residue of consumption', while denying others the use of this exploitation. Stimulated by the incursion of European capital into industrial life, which awakens national consciousness, even the colonial territories lose their pre-capitalist character and rebel against the dominance of the motherland. While the European foundation of the imperialistic advance grows ever broader, the pre-capitalist space of the world becomes increasingly smaller, unequally

3 Rosa Luxemburg: 'Accumulation of Kapitals' or 'What Have Epigons Done with the Marx's Theory'. An Anti-Criticism. Frankes Verlag in Leipzig, Page 18.

divided among states that have adopted their own industry in capitalist form, long after others have already seized significant portions of the Earth. The future must thus bring us a new cycle of crises, from which arises 'the inevitability of war between actively imperialistic states' (Page 299), indeed a 'bundle of imperialist wars', whose deepest roots spring from the already 'visible disproportionality between the non-capitalist territories of individual capitalist states and their expansion necessities'.

The 'inescapable residue of consumption' – which eluded the keen eye of Marx, who considered the conditions of expanded reproduction under the assumption of a purely capitalist milieu where disruptions should be most evident – becomes in Sternberg's exposition a scourge upon humanity of no lesser force and magnitude than, in Rosa Luxemburg's view, the entire mass of surplus value destined for accumulation, requiring the involvement of 'third parties' for purchase. The 'mass' dwindled to the 'residue'; but is what remains now truly of indestructible nature?

The capitalist original sin begins, according to Sternberg, with the export of consumer goods to a pre-capitalist economy. Here, they are either paid for with other consumer goods, whose consumption within the motherland indicates that they were not unabsorbable as value measures but were not sought after in a given natural form, or exchanged for raw materials that flow into the industry of the motherland. The entrepreneurs who produce means of production, semi-finished goods, etc. (Department 1 of Marx's schemes of expanded reproduction), and who can now import because the finished goods entrepreneurs (Department 2) have exported, become debtors to the latter, who become creditors of Department 1. The unabsorbable residue of consumption is thus invested in the means of production industry through the detour of the colonial land. This detour is not 'logically necessary', meaning it has no economic connection with an unabsorbable value measure and will only occur in reality if, on-site, the natural conditions for expanding raw material production or correspondingly cheap labour are lacking. And just as well, this transaction could be situated in the processing industry!

Sternberg only sees the exchange of finished products from the motherland for raw materials from the colonial countries, but he is not clear about its economic significance, about the granting of credit that is included here. He vehemently dismisses the assumption that accumulated profits flow back and forth between different spheres of production, for instance, that a shoe manufacturer could buy shares in a dynamo factory, because the entire Marxist method is precisely based on the idea that the sale of individual commodities is only possible through the exchange between these two departments (Page 99). However, this is not a matter of questions regarding the Marxist method, but at most about 'the systematic inclusion of facts neglected by Marx into the analysis of the capitalist process', which Sternberg promises us in the preface, and the 'living Marx' that he desires on his side! Now he would rather conjure 'a whole bundle of imperialist wars' upon us instead of including credit – which in the latest stage of capitalism, the stage of finance capital, is one of the most important aspects, into the study of crises – all because Marx's schemas were based on cash payments? Yet, if Sternberg wants to avoid considering credit granted from Department 2 to Department 1 out of fear that it would overturn the entire Marxist method, he still sneaks credit in. And he must do so, for otherwise, he would have to give away or let deteriorate part of the consumer goods in the colonies.

Sternberg presents another argument against the assumption that the accumulated surplus value of Department 2, namely consumer goods in their natural form, can be utilised in Department 1: 'You can't build machines with stearin candles'. (Page 28)

Sternberg is entirely correct in recognising the technical constraints of production here, but it must not be forgotten that with the worker's wages, alongside sausages and shoes, 'stearin candles' can also be purchased at times! Shifting the 'stearin candles' to Department 1 thus, according to the Marxian method, implies that they do not illuminate the hut of a Hindu, but are bought in the thoroughly capitalised motherland with the variable capital of the means of production industry – thereby causing the unabsorbable residue of consumption to disappear. Natural conditions for the establishment or expansion of an industry can be lacking and must then be compensated for through exchange. 'Different communities find different means of production and different foods in their natural environment. Their mode of production, way of life, and products are therefore diverse. It is this naturally occurring diversity that, when communities come into contact, gives rise to the exchange of their mutual products as commodities. Exchange does not create the differentiation of production spheres; rather, it brings the different spheres into contact and transforms them into more or less interdependent branches of a societal total production. It is here that the social division of labour arises through exchange of originally distinct but mutually independent spheres of production'.[4]

The exchange of mutual products grows with the development of large-scale industry, which selects its location based on either raw materials (such as coal, for instance) and relies on the procurement of constantly increasing quantities of materials (English cotton industry), or on the availability of labour, trade

4 Marx: 'Capital', Vol. 1, Page 298. Volksausgabe Stuttgart, 1914.

routes, and foreign sources for both raw materials and materials (Swiss, Italian mechanical engineering industry). Since American cotton came to England from the outset not as tribute but as a commodity, its import had to be paid for with exports regardless of the size of the non-capitalist space. With the disappearance of the internal, non-capitalist space, English exports steadily increased, as now food imports also had to be paid for. The English Department 2 – the Marxist consumer goods industry – cannot supply the market with grain or livestock, even if it provides cakes and meat preserves! 'Third parties' henceforth must not only take over Sternberg's entire 'unabsorbable residue of consumption', not only the entire value portion destined for accumulation in Rosa's English economy, but a quantum of export goods, the enormous scale of which was determined by the massive figures of England's deficits in food and raw materials. A significant portion of circulating capital (wages, raw and auxiliary materials) could now find its way back to realisation only through the detour of countries that have a surplus of grain, meat, fat, wool, wood, cotton, i.e., agricultural countries, whether colonial in character or not.

Now, England required 'third parties', but the role assigned to them was not to replace the lacking purchasing power domestically, nor to cover the 'overarching pinnacle of productive power', but simply to balance the inherent diversity of mutual products that had been further intensified by the displacement of the farmer.

The English trade balance became strongly passive in this regard – the total value of imports has consistently exceeded export values since the mid-nineteenth century, which even 'the dullest eye', to which Sternberg frequently appeals, should indicate that the necessity of exports here does not stem from an absolute lack of purchasing power or flawed value proportions.[5] The domestic industry in England must already engage in substantial exports to pay off raw material debts, while the demand from food importers for foreign exchange encourages and facilitates their other exports.

The same compulsion toward foreign trade exists for all states whose industry relies on foreign raw materials or auxiliaries, as well as for all agricultural states with pre-capitalist economies where domestic industry fails to supply agricultural tools, machinery, textiles to the desired extent. This holds true for England as much as it does for Soviet Russia. In foreign trade, it is not a specific form of social appropriation that comes into play, but a particular form of social division of labour. This has been noted by bourgeois economists like Rosa Luxemburg, but it was equally observed by Marx. However, while in

5 Vergleiche Helene Bauer: "The Imperial War", Kampf, Band 17.

primitive societies the social division of labour arises 'through the exchange of originally distinct but mutually independent spheres of production', in the era of capitalist large-scale industry, individual national spheres of production are already interdependent and intertwined from their very inception. Exchange now enables the existence of many industrial branches (European cotton industry, North American rubber industry), and as a consequence, a trade in commodities must further ensue, regardless of the mode of production and distribution. In the competitive struggle, capital seeks to vanquish its rivals through mass production, concentrating all its force on specific industrial sectors, neglecting others. As a result, it often appears in the wake of increased exports, which tempts economic theorists to attribute phenomena that partly arise from its technology to its mode of appropriation. Import, in the meantime, is mostly trivialised or entirely overlooked: in the shadow of the exporter, theory fails to perceive the importer, who is constantly present and often combines both functions in practice. Likewise, Sternberg aims to relieve the domestic market through commodity exports and capital expansion. However, the importer brings different goods as equivalents and interest payments into the country. What happens now? Does a crisis erupt? No, quite the opposite. We read: 'because capital returns in the form of previously exported interest payments, capital export allows for a higher standard of labour productivity!'

However, even if crises do not necessarily emerge from the conditions of expanded reproduction, they do break out in the reality of the economy with all their dreadful consequences! Capitalism fulfills its historical mission, the creation of the world market, only in a contradictory, flawed manner. Everything that is interdependent, and even already intertwined, appears independent, acts out of petty group and individual interests, seeks to barricade its own house, and hopes to encounter open doors everywhere immediately. The necessary value and quantity relations of various branches of labour are adjusted to each other only through intense bargaining in the world markets and through smaller negotiations in the national markets for goods, capital, and labour. However, the juggling of anarchic elements surely cannot bring the individual elements of the global economy into the equilibrium conditions of the Marxist schemas! The proportions are poorly chosen – new ones must be found amidst the crisis of demand!

Sternberg's book, vivid, witty, and passionate, albeit flawed in its structure and exacerbating every error, is nonetheless necessary, indeed 'logically necessary'. The 'unabsorbable residue of consumption', the 'economic roots of imperialism', the 'inapplicability of wars in the era of advanced capitalism', all of these notions linger in many minds. That the World War arose from the crimes and recklessness of military cliques, from the dynastic interests of the Habsburgs, from the megalomania of Wilhelm II, from the prestige politics of the Romanovs, many cannot reconcile with the usual, primitive type of materialistic view of history that asks about economic interests rather than socio-economic causality. Instead of analysing the social relations in which the arbitrariness of individuals could still bring about the most significant decisions, they fixate on the English and German export figures, which merely indicate that highly industrialised countries engage in trade among themselves as well as with agrarian nations, revealing their interconnectedness to the hilt! Capitalism, in alliance with feudal powers, can be bellicose, aiming to increase its profit rate through war and by means of war. However, it can also be peaceful. Instead of resorting to armed force, it can use state-backed credit guarantees for dealings with countries whose legal conditions arouse suspicion, thereby gaining new markets. It can strive for profit assurance through international cartels, quota allocation, and other means. Yet, within the anarchy of the mode of production, none of these methods is suitable to eliminate crises. Likewise, the possession of colonies, which can no longer be coerced into accepting unwanted goods through military might, cannot make them disappear.

England, with its extensive colonial holdings and agrarian constituent states, has just as many unemployed as Germany, which has had to relinquish its costly colonies. Sternberg presents the fanatics of imperialist war with their own thoughts in grotesque distortion, scrutinises them from all angles, marshals rich statistical material, and can seize upon the 'unabsorbable residue of consumption', simply because according to Marx's method, profits must always be reinvested in the same sphere of production where they originate. However, capitalists do not adhere to what Sternberg mistakenly considers the Marxist method. They choose the investment sphere from which a higher profit rate beckons, whether domestic or foreign, and avail themselves of both investment and distribution credits. This also makes the 'consumption residue' disappear – at least on paper. Yet, in the aimless mode of capitalist production, there will always be unsalable goods, idle means of production, and a lack of purchasing power among the broad strata whose labour is not *cultivated* but exploited and squandered. *It is not the abolition of mere capitalist private property but rather socialist planned economy that can bring about change here.*

CHAPTER 15

Accumulation, Credit, Imperialism (1927), Vol. 4: 173–9

The course of capitalist development is not characterised by uniform organic growth, but boom and crisis, a sudden flurry of industrial and commercial activity, as if rushing towards the bus stop on a newly emerging track, only to be stopped and thrown back, then to go further than what was previously achieved. The prospect of a quiet building on the foundations that an earlier economic epoch provisioned as a promise for the future, as well as a commitment to the future in terms of stocks of raw materials, tools, machines, and luxury foods, derived from 'saved', i.e. accumulated goods, such as goods and money capital, is not in sight right now. Capital goes beyond its own limits in the business cycle and even if every concrete development process seems to rest on the previous development, the past does not play a commanding role in the flexible economic process of modern society. Certainly, at the beginning of the year, one can only bring into the factories those machines that were completed at the end of the previous one, and in this sense, the volume of the newly acquired technical apparatus determines the rate at which production can be expanded. However, the extent to which the existing production means can be utilised can be shifted to such an extent that industrial activity can be significantly expanded at any given moment, even without any augmentation in the existing factory facilities, engines, and machines. The extension of the working day by 1 to 2 hours per day, coupled with the implementation of double and triple work shifts, the utilisation of the existing labour force and available work equipment in a reinforced straight line, can compensate for the absence of accumulation for a prolonged period, and adapt the range of technical services to the increased demand. In mining, too, the surplus of products that has become necessary for industrial purposes can be achieved to a considerable extent without any surplus of constant capital (tangible capital). The object of work is provided here without charge, and a mere increase in work translates directly into an increased mass of products, without any significant accumulation having to precede it. In agriculture, it is possible to achieve a larger quantity of grain, fibre, and oil plants without any capital contribution through an increased amount of work, better crop rotation, and more careful selection of seeds. *'By incorporating the two archetypes of wealth, labour, and land, capital acquires a resilience that allows it to expand the elements of its accumulation beyond the limits seemingly imposed by its own size, bound by the value and bulk of those already produced means of production in which it has its existence'.*[1]

The degree of flexibility between the magnitude of the total social production, which appears to be prepared and conditioned by the provision of supplementary construction facilities, machines, raw materials, and consumer goods, wherein the 'saved' portions of the profit intended for accumulation are embodied, and the respective possible 'unconditional' expansion of productive activity through the mere utilisation of such additional labour power or through the interaction of man and nature is so flexible that economic upswing is, in fact, never rendered impracticable by solely technical obstacles. It is always possible to create new streams of goods from new sources of raw materials, and new workers can always appear on the market for commodities with additional demand.[2]

A given technical endpoint of the economy never precisely determines the coming morning because its possibilities lie not in the mass of existing capital but in the size of the available workforce and the natural conditions. While one can accurately describe the endpoint and determine the numerical relationship between constant and variable capital (goods and labour wages) or between different industries, no definite statements can be made about what follows, as a new relationship can arise from any point through increased labour effort. An answer to the question of how much the entire production or means of production industry of a given size will be able to claim in terms of consumer goods for its workers and capitalists, that is, what they will be able to buy with their wages and profits, can only be determined on a case-by-case basis, mostly relying on economic forecasting, and such a forecast can only have a limited value.

The consumption remainder calculated from an endpoint, which Fritz Sternberg claims to be absolutely non-marketable, unsellable, and therefore driving the push for imperialism within the capitalist nexus, is a chimera.[3]

---

1 Marx, *Kapital*, Band 1, Abschnitt XVII: *der Akkumulationsprozess des Kapitals*, Seite 569, Volksausgabe.

2 'Every advancement in chemistry increases the number of useful substances and the applications of those already known which, in turn, expands capital investment areas. He teaches how to recycle the waste from the production and consumption processes, *thereby generating fresh capital without committing any initial capital. Similar to the heightened exploitation of the natural resources through the mere increase in labour force intensity, science and technology are forces of expansion independent of the size of the functioning capital*'. (Italics by me. H.B) Marx, a.a.D., page 569.

3 Fritz Sternberg, '*Der Imperialismus*' in '*Der Kampf*', March 1927. Compare Helene Bauer, '*Der Imperialismus*' in '*Der Kampf*', January 1927. Page 9 on page 11 should read correctly: 'we see:

Although the expansion of production beyond the limits of the already accumulated capital is always technically possible, it appears to be economically tied to the availability of additional sums of money with which workers can be paid and raw materials can be purchased. The money at the disposal of the capitalist entrepreneur comes to him from the market, from the proceeds of the sold goods, and represents the value of the goods he has already produced and thrown into the cycle of goods. His profit corresponds – at a given profit rate – precisely to the size of his production capacity, and since his ability to save is limited to his profit, any possibility for him to expand operations, create something new in the future, is already limited in advance by the scope of his previous production. If he hasn't produced more, sold more, and profited more in the past, then he cannot move forward at a faster pace than before, and the past seems to lead calmly and steadily into the future – without boom, high demand, or crisis.

The idea that, in a capitalist society, an individual can only dispose of other people's goods or services if he has acquired purchasing power through the previous sale of his own is rooted in the old days of bartering in kind to which some people still cling.

Every purchase to the extent of selling is a goods exchange, albeit mediated by money, while the secret of modern profiteering does not lie in exchange but in command over elements of production. In the period of expansion, the capitalist entrepreneur does not possess the full equivalent value for the labour force, raw materials, and auxiliary means he withdraws from the market, nor can he possess it before the completion of the new production period because it does not yet exist and must be produced first. Until that time, he must draw goods that serve as the initiation of production without any real reciprocation, that is, he must take credit.

The credit provided by modern credit banks to industry, that is, operating and investment credit, is, apart from the real savings deposits (which do not play a significant role), a creation of new purchasing power. The additional means of payment obtained by the credit recipient from the bank and introduced into circulation 'are, by their nature, certificates of future services and goods yet to be produced … these are means of payment for which, initially, nothing corresponds – at least no contribution to the social product, although in practice, this deficiency is often filled by other things'.[4] (Credit-worthiness!)

Because interest flows back from the earlier capital exports, the export of capital allows for the higher living standard of the working class'.

4 Josef Schumpeter, 'Theorie der volkswirtschaftlichen Entwicklung'. Seite 147. Zweite, neu bearbeitete Auflage. Verlag von Dunker und Humblot, 1926.

Credit does not only discount 'the later purchase', as Sternberg suggests, but 'it mediates the actual successive phases of production of the same article'.[5] And it makes the production of goods, with which the various creditors are subsequently paid and whose ownership the bank transfers to the entrepreneurs, possible in the first place. The modern economy is inherently 'constantly liquid' because, assuming private property and extensive division of labour, the material can only be taken up to higher stages of processing with the crutch of credit.[6] 'Lend capital and industrial capital are identical here', says Marx.[7] Until the final product is available, its distribution, that is, eventual payment to all those who have provided the necessary raw materials and production means for its production, is impossible.

Those, like Sternberg, who assume that a commodity is unsaleable because they cannot spot a ready-to-exchange counterpart in their vicinity, confuse in their thinking the modern process of circulation, which is merely a lever of production and distribution, with the exchange of primitives!

Marx thoroughly investigated all the factors that lead to the expansion of capitalist production beyond the limits of constant capital, the role of credit in the expansion of industrial and commercial activities, and the changes in demand and exchange relations from all angles, teaching us to recognise in all conditions of upswing the necessary conditions for its abrupt termination. The reproduction on an extended scale is driven forward in the unplanned capitalist economy by changes in exchange relations, continuously generating new ones, and thus its connection with the phenomenon of crises is established.

But the schematic representation of accumulation in the second volume of *Capital* abstracts from all the moments that are most intimately connected with the essence of the capitalist development process.

There is no cyclical unfolding of soaring ups and downs here, but constant growth. Here, no technical innovation changes the relationship between constant and variable capital, and no price shift disturbs the exchange relations of the beginning. Every quantity of goods is exchanged for a finished quantity of goods of the same value. The technical design of the expanded production is strictly prescribed by the capitalists by the mass of means of production completed with every turnover of capital. The same Marx who emphatically points out that accumulation is not bound by the limits of technology seems to know

5 Marx, a.a.D., Vol. 3/2, P. 19.

6 Compare Albert Hahn, 'Volkswirtschaftliche Theorie des Bankkredits', Von Mohr Publishers, Tübingen, 1924.

7 Ibid, p. 18.

nothing of this in the analysis of the schematic conditions of extended reproduction – not even of the role of credit.

Fritz Sternberg believes that, if Marx 'only analyses the exchange of commodities at this point, he is absolutely correct' (p. 122) Yes, but the methodical correctness of Marx's approach lies precisely in the fact that he not only considered credit but also all other well-known facts, such as the change in organic composition, rising raw material prices, increased utilisation of machinery, overtime, wage increases, etc. at the same time. Thus, it is also evident that Marx did not intend to capture the entire process of capitalist development, the inner laws of which he was the first to recognise and incorporate into economic theory, in a numerical framework. Instead, he aimed to illustrate and comprehend the *interrelated relationships* that arise from the fragmentation of the social economic body into seemingly independent yet interconnected and mutually dependent production branches.

Closeness to reality can only be achieved by systematically including all the moments that Marx left out of consideration, one after another, or by simply accepting them as they are and for what they are. That's a lot, an enormous amount, but it's not a reflection of the pulsating life, like all the hundreds of pages of *Capital* that precede the 'schematic presentation of accumulation' and all the others that follow. Fritz Sternberg is determined to improve the schemes and, without any apparent reason, adds a randomly selected element simply because it's missing, thereby excluding other possibilities of variation, since Marx didn't employ them, and thus halting the slowly but steadily advancing cart. He complicates the conditions of exchange because they are more complicated in reality than they are in the schemes, keeps credit away from them 'because the whole Marx method is based on the fact that individual commodities can only be sold through exchange between the two departments' and in this way gets leftover goods THAT push for imperialist advances, since they cannot be sold within the creditless capital nexus and makes the unsaleable by necessity.

In every phase of capitalism, technical progress, the development towards an ever-higher organic composition of capital, the percentage increase in the means of production apparatus, etc. are all normal. Credit, the expansion of note circulation, the rise in interest rates, etc., are all normal. A schema is always accidental, depending on the particular purpose of the presentation to single out one thing from the abundance of facts and to leave the other unconsidered, for practical purposes – and Sternberg's book wants to be practical. A cropped reality is not useful for practical purposes.

And only in reality that has been trimmed down in this way does imperialism become a vital necessity for the capital of the industrialised countries!

The word 'imperialism' has an almost magical appeal to many minds. At the sound of it, the thousands of intertwined relationships between the free states, which in their rich abundance almost combine to form a common economic body, fade immediately, and the export of capital to the colonial countries becomes an ever-freshly bubbling source of wealth. But the export of capital – that is, a gift of goods (i.e. of a service) without direct consideration – only increases the stock of goods of the taker, not of the giver, and can never result in an increase in the standard of living in the exporting country. The exported values remain in the possession of the capitalist class, but they are lost to the accumulation of the mother country, to the demand for labour. This can be seen clearly in France, Europe's largest creditor state at the time before the world war. Here, the strong export of capital inhibited the development of large-scale industry, and despite the weak population development, wages and general working conditions were less favourable than in Germany, for example. The French working class was not given an advantage by the capital expansion, because the grace period that imperialism granted the workers belongs, according to Sternberg, to the realm of illusions of power with which the bourgeoisie's lordlings otherwise feed the public. The English working class does not owe the favourable structure of their real wages to English capital exports, but to the lead of English industry (which for a long time secured it a monopoly-like character), strong emigration, trade union affiliation, and the duty-free supply of all important foodstuffs. England has abandoned its agricultural pursuits and has emerged as the premier purchaser of agricultural commodities from its overseas states and colonies. This also puts the English trader in a favourable position in the global market competition. Between 1909 and 1913, England on its own imported as much wheat on average as Germany, Belgium, France, and Austria together.[8] And here lies the secret of England's good sales prospects.

Sternberg sees the high numbers of English exports as proof 'that England had an advantage over its competitors simply by seizing political power, by converting the ownerless, non-capitalist space into a colonial space' (o.d., p. 412). But the sale of English goods in the colonies does not take place under political pressure, any more than the sale of wheat from Canada or wool from Australia does in England. The per capita export value in 1913 was 284 gold marks for Great Britain, 288 for Switzerland, 288 for Denmark, and 275 for Argentina, and Norway and Sweden were able to export significantly more in relation to the size of the population than France with its extensive colonial posses-

8 Reinhard, '*Weltwirtschaftliche und politische Erdkunde*', Breslau, 1925.

sions.[9] The domination of colonial territories does not seem to be a necessary condition for the size of the export trade!

The extensive compilation of numbers that Sternberg assembles regarding the size of English commerce with the overseas territories is well known. They were eagerly circulated in Imperial Germany in connection with the naval bill and served to create an atmosphere for colonial policy, whose boon for the economy of the mother country they allegedly prove. Alongside traders and industrialists, who didn't really want to go along with it, German workers should also have learned from these numbers that warships were the most important instrument of national welfare. Sternberg tries to underpin these teachings in a Marxist way, and believes that he is thereby strengthening the international solidarity of the working class and being able to render a service to the revolution. But it seems to me that he made a wrong choice of weapons.

Fascists' noisy, imperialistic rhetoric is just as little an expression of the economic necessity of the capital as were the speeches of Wilhelm II, although they were followed by the world war.[10] Certainly, fascism is just as socially conditioned as the position of the dynasty in old Germany and in the Danube monarchy, but neither the world conflagration of 1914 to 1918 nor the unrest and ferment of the post-war period can be explained by capital's urge to expand. The collapse of European colonial rule would not constrain the world economy, but would in all probability bring it to a much higher level of development, for the political shackles, which in an earlier epoch were certainly an effective if also brutal means to force the Tropes in the world economy are now only an obstacle to the economic development of the controlled areas. Strong national governments in the Far East are currently tasked with the responsibility of establishing modern administrations. They must explore means of procuring by utilising all sources of raw materials and promoting the export of all products from the exotic plant world, for which there is a need in Europe and America. The per capita import of goods in 1925 was 14 gold marks in British India, seven in China, and 74 gold marks in industrially highly developed Japan! New forms of life create new needs and result in increased imports and exports of goods, albeit after a longer or shorter transitional period. The political repression that creates the compulsion to work more prevents the transition to better, more productive work – to better performance and new needs.

Imperialism offers no protection against the crisis, which contains many sources of conflict and new serious dangers of war, but it does not mean a

9 'Economic State Yearbook 1925', published by the Chamber for Workers and Employees in Vienna.

10 Wilhelm Ellenbogen, *'Faschismus und Kriegsgefahr'*. 'der Kampf', März 1927.

permanent crisis or even a sinking into barbarism according to any capitalist law either. The populists of all nations call for more place in the sun to carve out more place for themselves in the state crib, and find a secret ally in the intelligentsia's drive for power and prestige, which is awake everywhere, in the romantic magic of distance and in the greed for profit of the suppliers of war. Imperialism thrives on instinctual feelings, on slogans, on phrases that seek to veil class antagonisms with the veil of dreams of power. Unveiling them by analysing the economic and physical factors of imperialism is also one of the tasks of the Marxist school in this case.

CHAPTER 16

Economic Upswing and Fascism, *Der Kampf* (1936), Vol. 12: 469–74

The rise in prices of all raw materials on global markets, the shrinking world reserves of food, colour, textiles, and the reduction of import restrictions – which were meant to defend prices during the crisis by throttling both supply and production of primary products – along with the high figures published to illustrate the economic situation concerning industrial production in general or the flourishing state of individual sectors, all together paint a picture of a strong economic upswing. Captured and measured in global economic statistics, capitalism appears to be rapidly regaining its pre-crisis position and, although not yet reflecting the full glory of the record year 1929, it has certainly reached a proximity to it. According to the report from the League of Nations, industrial activity in the capitalist world in 1935 was only 13 percent below that of 1929. The improvement is evident, with each passing year showing a recovery from the crisis low of 1932 that was stronger than the corresponding time of the previous year. In 1935, it was 10 percent against the previous year and is likely to have maintained that accelerated pace in 1936 as well.

In the debate over the interpretation of the global economic crisis, those who see it not as the definitive collapse of capitalism against the cliffs of its own contradictions, but merely as a cyclical downturn, seem to be vindicated. They argue that despite its gigantic scale, this crisis, like previous ones, will be overcome by the inherent upward forces of capitalism triggered by its own automatism.

However, the belief in a capitalist recovery from the crisis is significantly shaken by the peculiar nature of the phenomena that are now collectively referred to as the economic upswing of the world economy. While industrial value creation has risen significantly since the depths of the crisis, the improvement is distributed unevenly across different sectors. Many countries have already reached or even surpassed their levels of industrial production from 1929 by twenty, thirty percent or more, while others still lag considerably behind.

We see a strong increase in industrial production, particularly in many agrarian states such as Hungary, Greece, Finland, and Yugoslavia. The collapse of raw material prices here sparked efforts to create new employment opportunities for the population through the establishment of industries. These industrial foundations during the crisis were not a reckless surge of optimism, nor a blossoming and flourishing; rather, they represented a difficult struggle against foreign exchange shortages and unemployment. The collapse of agricultural and raw material prices reduced their access to foreign currency, which simultaneously robbed the capital-weak agrarian countries of international credit and also of foreign financial assistance. The foreign loans that had previously powerfully promoted the industrialisation of agricultural areas were no longer available. Foreign assistance had to be replaced by state aid, which brought increased tariff protection, subsidies, tax pressure, and wage pressure.

In contrast to Russia, where the focus was first on the production of its own means of production industries and only on that basis expanded consumer goods production, the new establishments in agrarian countries, with modest investment possibilities, primarily produced for direct mass consumption, such as textiles, footwear, leather, wood products, and light industry. Some sales channels were thus shifted away from the old industrial countries. For example, due to the new establishments, the textile industry in its traditional locations, such as England, Czechoslovakia, Belgium, and Switzerland, has entered a state of chronic crisis, as evidenced by efforts in England to swiftly eliminate 10 million spindles, and in France and Czechoslovakia to halt the decline through forced consolidation. The cotton industry, which expanded significantly during the crisis in Japan and the United States, along with the new wool industry in Australia, is now permanently changing the landscape of European textile goods on the world market.

In the old industrial countries, efforts were simultaneously made to find replacements for the foreign sales lost due to the direct and indirect effects of the crisis. This was achieved by introducing new types of production, encouraging agriculture, and increasing the production of meat, milk, and butter. From 1928 to 1934, wheat production in European grain-importing countries decreased by 20 percent, while at the same time, it decreased in the Danube region and in overseas areas by a similar amount. The planned reduction of grain farming on one hand and its promotion on the other caused staple grains like bread wheat and sugar to lose their previous significance in the world market. Throughout the crisis, economies rapidly sought to fill the gaps created by the contraction of exports by expanding domestic production. The costs of unemployment insurance made high protective tariffs, subsidies to industry and agriculture, and increased commodity prices appear economically justifiable, as long as they could positively affect the labour market. Where high unemployment was accompanied by distress and a lack of credit, everything that saved cash payments to foreign countries was considered economically sensible. The import of finished goods was reduced in favour of semi-finished products, and the import of semi-finished products was reduced in favour of raw materials, while domestic production of various substitute materials, such as artificial textile fibres and fuels made from wool or wood, was promoted. The structural changes that resulted in the economies of individual states are now reflected in the altered structure of world trade. While the quantity of raw materials traded in 1935 reached 93.5 percent of its weight from 1929, the recovery of world trade in food only reached 86 percent, and in finished goods, it only reached 68.5 percent of the 1929 level. During this period, Europe's share of international trade in goods significantly decreased.

In response to the necessary shifts within the economies due to the pressure of the crisis, the state had to step in, as long-term loans for investment purposes were unavailable. The state became a refuge. Farmers, who could no longer sustain themselves from their land due to significantly reduced earnings, entrepreneurs facing declining demand in domestic and foreign markets, and the unemployed seeking jobs all turned to the state. And the state responded. Through support, rehabilitation, and promotional actions, along with monetary and trade policy experiments. The state's interventions in the economy created an outward appearance of a war of all against all, further burdened by general currency insecurity following the devaluation of the pound and the dollar. Internally, this led to bureaucratic, more or less unplanned, and variously tiered management of the economy by the state. In Italy and Germany, the fascist great powers, this resulted in a transformation and control of the economy by the state, now characterised by a high level of employment.

The economy of a fascist great power exhibits entirely different characteristics than statism, which consists of the isolated, uncoordinated, and mostly improvised economic interventions of the state in small countries that oscillate between parliamentarism and dictatorship. The fascist dictatorship of a great power aims to suppress and subdue social tensions through an imperialist ideology, labeling class fighters as traitors to the state. Therefore, it must proclaim revenge, war, and conquest as state purposes. The stirring up of national and racist sentiments, the imminent threat of war, and the psychological experience of it are intended to fend off the encroachment of 'Marxism' and to secure the exploitation of the working class, which serves the fascist alliance of heavy industry, the nobility, the army, and declassed adventurers for all time.

Mussolini soon demonstrated a keen interest in expanding agricultural and industrial production after securing his power. Large swamp areas were drained, the cotton and artificial silk industries were significantly expanded, and the automotive, aviation, and machine-building industries experienced rapid growth, with the entire country being explored for coal, ore, and bauxite deposits. The establishment of new industrial enterprises continued even after the outbreak of the world crisis and amidst a substantial decrease in foreign currency inflow. This period saw the extreme exploitation of foreign credit, and when the credit bubble collapsed due to the rebellion of creditors, nearly the entire gold reserve was sacrificed for the industrialisation of the country, which was now clearly beginning to serve war armament and preparation. Through rapidly successive internal loans, the state absorbed all newly accumulated funds in the country until, ultimately, the nationalisation of central banks turned the credit system into a branch of public administration.

The state can now steer the country's economy along the paths it desires by appropriately distributing credit without having to pose a confidence question through the issuance of bonds. The state-controlled corporations decide on additional imports and exports, while strict foreign exchange management and the confiscation of all foreign assets by the state cut off any possibility of private trade relations with abroad. The Abyssinian War led to further measures for directing and monitoring production, consumption, and prices. These measures have not been lifted even after the war.

The major industries of Italy, namely the metal and textile industries, have long been entirely supplied by foreign raw materials. With the increasing scarcity of foreign currency, the effort intensified to save on import currencies by producing domestic substitutes and exploiting even the lowest-quality coal, oil, and ore deposits that are costly to process. The profitability of these economically irrational enterprises is ensured by state contracts, state subsidies, and the prohibition of strikes.

Hitler's Germany, like Mussolini's Italy, presents the image of an economy being led through dictatorship towards the highest state of military readiness. Through compulsory loans from financial institutions and the prohibition of private emissions, the state absorbs the liquid assets of the market and channels them to industries of 'highest state importance'. The less important sectors are kept deliberately tight through investment bans, restrictions on new enterprises, and expansion prohibitions. State contracts secure the profitability of heavy industry, automobile and aircraft factories, armament and machinery manufacturing, as well as electrical and chemical capital, while the consumer goods industries are not allowed to renew their machinery and are forced into short-time work due to a shortage of raw materials, leading to technical and economic decline. The requirement for approval for imports and exports, along with foreign exchange management and compensation agreements, collectively form a decentralised foreign trade monopoly. Ultimately, state authorities determine the quality and quantity of goods that enter the exchange, the industry groups that are to be supplied with raw materials and semi-finished products, and the goods whose production is throttled in favour of others. The self-help of enterprises deemed less important for state purposes is nearly excluded due to the state agencies' control over all domestic and foreign raw materials. All agricultural products from the country are directed through mandatory delivery to the collection points of the Reichsnähramt, supplied to wholesalers according to official dispositions, and distributed in fixed quantities to small retailers. The Reichsnähramt sets prices and trade margins.

The German substitute materials economy, into which the Third Reich has slipped, is now being expanded and deepened with the proclamation of the Second Four-Year Plan, developed with dictatorial force. The cheaper and more abundant standard of living that the former German refinement trade with foreign countries aimed for is now being replaced by the state-imposed struggle for an expensive autarky, intended to sustain a war with a still uncertain front and unreliable allies. Natural products from foreign zones, which are available in any quantity on the world markets, are being produced in the country at an enormous cost of labour and capital. The price of finished goods will bear the high raw material prices, and despite the exertion of all economic forces, supply remains tight and inadequate.

The largest profits of the favoured industries are now being used partly on direct orders from the state and partly through the bond route to expand the substitute materials economy. The most powerful financial and industrial groups are becoming increasingly tied to the autarky and to the regime that imposes it. For the producers of substitute materials, the substitute materials economy is as economically sound as the production of weapons of murder for the armaments magnates. However, any loosening of the restraints imposed on German foreign trade could undermine and devalue the substitute materials capital. Autarky cannot fill the food gaps or the most significant gaps in the German metal industry copper, nickel, tin, manganese, and so on – and the loosening of economic relations with foreign countries that it entails threatens the German Reich with the loss of sales channels, which are essential for continuing rearmament and for food supply. The victorious battle with labour has brought food and raw material shortages to the Third Reich: further victories along the path of the Four-Year Plan – with still impressive production figures – lead into a dead end, at the end of which lies only the choice between war and retreat.

Foreign debt, raw material shortages, and currency crises have quickly matured certain organisations in both Germany and Italy, while others have been more sharply defined or prevented from emerging. However, the general structure of the trade relations of both states with foreign countries has its deepest roots not in the scarcity of resources, but in the nature of the fascist regime, which seeks to complement the control of the economic forces of the country through the regulation and management of foreign trade, analogous to the proletarian dictatorship.

Italy and Germany, two highly industrialised states with over 110 million inhabitants, have torn themselves away from the world economy through the systematic reorganisation of their economies from the perspective of a war-oriented state purpose, thereby also severing ties with the cyclical movement of capital beyond their borders. Large parts of their industries are in a flourishing state, and the number of unemployed is lower than in 1929. However, what we see there is not a capitalist upswing, but a fascist economy in high gear, making feverish preparations for war and endurance amid rising shortages of food and raw materials, with a disenfranchised and poorly paid workforce.

The fascism that is widely situated in the centre of the continent inevitably imprints its features on the economic face of Europe. By 1935, Europe already had a higher consumption of iron, copper, lead, aluminum, and tin than at the peak of the economic cycle in 1929. This economic revival takes on a peculiar character due to the unusually increased consumption of iron and non-ferrous metals. The entire Swedish armaments industry, which is 90 percent oriented toward exports, is operating at full capacity. The Bofors arms company, which reported an order backlog of 27 million Swedish kronor for 1934, received orders worth 82 million for the current year. The British steel and iron industry is operating at full capacity, fighting for the possibility of expansion, and taking in vast amounts of foreign raw materials. Leading enterprises are increasing their equity capital, acquiring smaller factories, and expanding in all directions. The armaments contracts, both for domestic and foreign accounts, are creating employment in the large sectors of the iron and metal industry everywhere, stimulating world trade through substantial shipments of metals that Europe needs for rearmament.

In England and Sweden, where the rearmament boom coincided with the housing activities strongly promoted by the governments, along with ample capital, low interest rates, and a incipient economic recovery, the armaments contracts were able to trigger a capitalist boom in which all industrial sectors are participating. The number of employees in both countries is higher than ever, and the cost of living for workers is continuously rising. Besides Sweden, Norway, Denmark, Finland, and Estonia are also involved in the capitalist upswing. The English market is again taking in significant quantities of food, and timber has become a highly sought-after and marketable commodity due to the revitalisation of shipbuilding activities. The newly established industries during the crisis are finding buyers in the domestic market. We also see new life in the long-deserted shipyards. In addition to the vessels intended for war fleets, new merchant ships and passenger ships are being constructed. For in America, life is now lively, and in the European metropolises, people are building gas-proof shelters and clearing out attics in anxious worry of air raids, but they are also preparing the large hotels and entertainment establishments for a new influx of dollar travellers from America with feel-good prosperity sentiments.

The overseas raw material-producing countries are recovering from the long depression due to rising world market prices for their products and are entering into a more active exchange of goods. However, continental Europe, with the exception of the Scandinavian countries, stands apart from this movement and often experiences only the negative aspects of the increasing demand for foreign currency. In this area, which is constantly held in check by political tensions, a severe depression still prevails, even though iron and steel production occupies a special position there, as for example in Czechoslovakia.

In the countries of the gold bloc, where a revival of export industries is now hoped for due to monetary policy measures, a new unemployment of no insignificant extent has emerged in the past three years. In Czechoslovakia, Belgium, the Netherlands, and Austria, the index of industrial production in June–July 1936 reached only between 74 and 78 percent of the level from the summer of 1929, with the Netherlands still even lower. In Czechoslovakia and Belgium, unemployment has significantly decreased over the last two years, while in Austria it continues to rage – but it remains high everywhere. In the fascist great powers, the battle with the labour has been won, but their labour slaves in the Third Reich now hear that their meagre wages are not to be improved any further, that the Four-Year Plan requires new sacrifices for the expansion of autarky, and they are suffering in Italy, where prices have quickly risen due to currency devaluation, from a new reduction in their rations.

The foreign trade of the two fascist great powers, shaped and constrained by autarky efforts, foreign currency shortages, and a lack of credit, adversely affects the economic development of all European states. It primarily forces the Southeast European countries to cling to many economically irrational and costly industrial establishments, to trade restrictions, and to an autarky imposed upon them by the disintegration of the European economic community. Mussolini's loud encouragement of Hungarian revisionism and Hitler's calls for a crusade against Bolshevism keep global capital at bay from these areas, which appear to the West as an uncertain, war-threatened ground due to the loquacity of the fascist leaders. There is no credit bridge from the rich countries experiencing a strong capitalist upturn – America, England, Scandinavia – to the capital-poor European states that lie within the sphere of interest of warring fascism.

The effects of fascism seem to want to exclude them from the economic upswing, at least until sufficient, peace-sustaining counterforces and alliances are organised.

CHAPTER 17

Marriage and Social Stratification, *Der Kampf*, (1927), Vol. 7: 319–24

A new marriage in the new state was a solution put forth by all utopians. Regardless of whether the external regulation of the social order was to be governed by the state, reason, or happiness as the supreme principle to which reality should serve, it always included the relationship between sexes within the realm of what needed to be regulated. This was done to align it with the chosen purpose and to bestow the best marriage as a necessary fulfillment.

The concept of development displaced the old dreams of philosophers and poets of an arbitrary shaping of social life – and created new ones. The course of history now appeared as a progression from lower to higher forms, as a unified process in which all of humanity is intricately entangled, more or less homogeneous. To minds schooled in evolutionism, the dominance of urban-industrial culture soon seemed to be the sole ruler, whose astonishing spread in England and rapid growth in Germany kept the immense expanse occupied by the peasant-petty-bourgeois mass (that is the European continent) veiled from view. It appeared as an unstoppable, naturally necessary culmination of an economic process, in which not only the old was pushed back, hollowed out, but also crushed and eradicated by the new. Development was now also attributed the role of fundamentally reshaping the relations between genders in its naturally necessary and lawful course, creating a new form of marriage in which the new economy and technology were to find a perfectly equivalent reflection. Here too, what had become historical was to be separated from history, in order to make room for the new and contemporary, enabling the new humans to navigate smoothly in the new world!

It was only through a strenuous struggle against the suggestive influence of the sociological perspective brought about by the age of inventions and the triumphant advent of large-scale mechanised enterprises that the realisation could prevail: the revolutionary practice of capital must come to a halt before forms of life that, despite their apparent weakness, are protected against its grasp due to their different nature of intention. The small-scale enterprise in the city and in the open countryside is not, for us, a low structure destined to roll into the darkness of the past with no space reserved for it in the world of the future. The city, to us, is no longer just composed of capitalists and proletarians. Development is no longer a current that sweeps away the viable, floods and washes away the useless, but rather an emergence of the new that is spurred on by the old, fighting to gain ground, and which must consequently yield a portion of the gained to the sprouting new growth. Decades and centuries collide: everything that has already taken on definite contours, that appears frozen, is deemed the past, while the gaze is cast toward the all-encompassing future in the fantastic chaos of what has emerged with us, and is rushing toward completion. But we are beginning to understand that there is a present in which the evolved and the evolving exist with equal rights – that we do not live between yesterday and tomorrow, but in a today of the most colorful diversity of life forms.

The economic landscape of the present, which we designate with the term 'capitalism', is richly structured into a juxtaposition and intermingling of old, new, and newest forms, which also coexist as a colorful mixture of cultural spheres even in the smallest nation-states. From this diversity of socio-economic foundations arises a diversity of ways of life, and consequently, a diversity of marriages that strongly vary in their meaning and content, but all still must be counted as part of the 'today'.

The peasant marriage, despite all the articles in the *Woman of Today Journal*, has been as little affected by change as peasant property and rural working methods. The house and the farm constitute the foundation for life and livelihood in the marriage, holding both the man and the woman captive in equal measure. For both, the 'economy', with all the joy and sorrow it offers, is the common object and goal of their work, care, and hope. Earning a living and maintaining the household form an inseparable unity here, and so the male and female spheres of work are scarcely separated and never entirely distinct – even though the woman may be more concerned with milk and poultry, while the man focuses on tilling the land. Labour and possession – guided by the wisdom of the ancestors in the choice of spouse, leading the son to marry a suitably prosperous woman – grant the woman a position within the peasant family where no semblance of economic dependency weighs upon her. She is a co-owner and collaborator, and she often manages the proceeds from the sale of milk, vegetables, eggs, etc., quite independently. After a few years of marriage, as the house and barn are expanded, possessions rounded out through acquisitions, and annual yields increased, it is also a few years of her life that, now integrated into the economy, begin to yield fruits. '*Bäuerin*' (farmer women) is not a title, but a dignity of work and a life's purpose that quickly merge so intimately with a plot of land that no human will can tear them apart. And the plot of land, beyond whose borders a foreign world already begins, belongs to the marriage through the alliance with the husband who, having spent as much of his life as the woman in the joint economy, ceases to be a 'farmer' when detached from his property. Here, the marriage is deeply rooted in the soil, thus becoming lasting and inseparable from its economic basis, offering no possibility of a peaceful way out for the wanderings and confusions of life.

The inseparability of the peasant marriage does not lie in external regulations by the city or the church, but in the farmer way of life, whose inner essence has been almost untouched by political and social revolutions up to now. Even the radical marriage law reform of Soviet Russia cannot change the weight of the peasant marriage, as it does not alter the socio-economic foundations of family life in the countryside.

Whether legislation makes divorce easier or impossible, the disruption of marriage in rural areas, if it cannot be overcome by compelling shared labour, will only be tragically borne and may find its epilogue in the court of law. For neither the farmer nor the farmer's wife willingly departs from their house and land.

Closely related to the peasant marriage, despite the external differences in circumstances, is the marriage in urban petty-bourgeois circles. The small shop or workshop connected to the residence forms the foundation for a marriage in which property and shared labour must unfold into a partnership of destiny. At the beginning of their independent existence, their meagre savings are pooled together for the first purchase of goods, for acquiring tools and materials, for setting up the workshop and home. The wife receives customers, collects payments, rises at dawn to buy in bulk the goods sold in small quantities during the day, manages the household and business as a shopkeeper or mistress. These activities fill her marriage.

The petty-bourgeois woman has never taken part in the women's movement, has never made independent demands on society. She creates and sustains her existence in partnership with her husband, together with him waging the difficult battle for survival of a class threatened by new technology and new organisational forms. Even though the guild system, unfortunately still remaining in many branches of work, makes it difficult or impossible for women to independently practice certain trades, she gains a strong share in the earnings through the wedding ring, and beyond that, she desires no other entitlement. While the golden era of craftsmanship has long passed, and apprentices have been separated from their absolute authority through legal protection and organisation, the master's wife still retains the dignity of the profession as a mistress. She navigates through tough times with clarity, her belief in being provided for through marriage remains, and faithfully she repeats the words she heard in her parental home: 'a woman belongs at home'.

The labour force of women here is to such a high degree a condition for the economic stability of the family and a complement to the husband's work that, in the fusion of gender and economic partnership, the petty- bourgeois marriage – like the peasant one – becomes a social entity, the dissolution of which resembles the destruction or deformity of something organic. In the close interconnection of earning a living, managing the household, and owning property, it is experienced through joint labour and generates an ideology that affirms marriage, possessing a strong economic foundation within the life order of petty-bourgeois strata. In this context, marriage is a task for both partners, which, despite all the difficulties arising from individual traits, must be fulfilled, as marital disruption easily co-destroys the material foundations of the family. Individual psychology, encompassing marital disruptions within the realm of therapeutic education and viewing attempts to break free from a spouse as a symptomatic failure of neurotics that could be mitigated through education about marriage and marriage counseling, appears as a scientific glorification of the vital necessity of the petty-bourgeois and peasant classes. Through marriage and within marriage, they assert their social existence, with their marital affirmation principle and the shifting of their issues into the realm of psychosis.

A seemingly similar affirmation of marriage can also be found among the upper echelons, where marriage ensures the legitimate heirs for the man and provides the woman with the corresponding social framework for inherited property. The arrangement of marriage laws is of no consequence to the spouses. Substantial wealth helps overcome many problems of marital union, it also surmounts legal barriers when marriage, despite the freedom that money provides, becomes a burden one wants to shed. The dissolution of marriage is merely an arrangement of financial matters, where nothing else needs to break apart, as the sparse functions that seem to lie within the family are already entrusted to outsiders.

Here, the woman leads a life of luxury, thereby perpetuating her socially passive behavior, giving the men of her class the illusion of being family providers. It is her duty to spend money on beauty, and the carefree manner in which she does so suggests that she is not deceived about the way it is acquired. She believes herself to be equally entitled to a share of the family provider's income, just as he is entitled to a share in the labour of the workers. She leeches off the leeches, and her political absence indicates that she does not consider her existence in need of reform.

The commitment to marriage is here a piece of tradition that one is reluctant to break without necessity. Conservatism, which seeks to bind others, and freedom, which money provides, prevent marriage and marital law from emerging as a problem in the most affluent circles, requiring the intervention of the state or society for its resolution.

The complexity of marriage only arises where traditionally inherited values clash with new living conditions – not among the old, but among the new urban strata, within bureaucracy and the liberal professions. Here, for the first time in history, women are pushed back into material dependence on men. The path to commodity, to the market, and therefore to independence, leads through monetary income – but income flows only to the man and the woman can only receive it through his work and from his hands! Earning a living is simultaneously separated from managing the household; both the intellectual and professional atmosphere of the man and the abundance of his vocational and societal connections remain inaccessible and foreign to the housewife. The recognition of her domestic duties rings hollow here; she senses the intellectual divide between men and women of her social stratum, observes the disdain of academics for those without higher education, and is aware of the meagre wage received by domestic helpers – the 'support' – for their housework. Yet, the domestic helper sustains herself, her work provides her with independent income over which she can freely dispose, while the housewife, with the wedding ring, merely gains the right to be maintained – a right that her children also have a claim to.

The bourgeois woman, whose home has become empty with the children's school readiness, the penniless girl from a good family who has long witnessed the maternal struggle for household income, the one excluded from free choice in love, gave rise to the women's movement. The goal was to establish a direct relationship between the bourgeois woman and society, separate from her state of unemployment, and to grant her access to all the means that, within her social stratum, signify full worth. Women became teachers, doctors, and now the path to all liberal professions is open to them. Marriage, which unites two people working together on the same endeavor among peasants and urban petty-bourgeois layers, in the city more frequently brings together two intellectual workers with separate spheres of influence, distinct professional interests, leading to separate social and friendship connections. The intellectual barrier between man and woman begins to soften – they grow more similar to each other under conditions that gradually alleviate the earthly weight of their marriage.

Strong childhood memories and the influence of inherited values still instill in the self-sufficient, active woman the aspiration to be a good housewife and mother. She still clings to many small domestic tasks and concerns, dedicates herself, both to convince herself and others, that her marriage is not essentially different from the good old marriage. She devotes much more time and attention to the matters of daily household life than the man, pushing her nerves to act as both woman and man simultaneously, which likely explains the rare occurrence of exceptional female achievements in professional fields. However, no matter how many nerves and time she dedicates to the household, her contribution is neither essential nor indispensable here.

Before the war, higher education for women was still a rarity – the impoverishment of the middle class due to the war and inflation has turned higher education for women, leading to independent earning, into a widespread phenomenon. Dowries must now be replaced across the board through personal earnings, which also provide the only means of securing one's existence! Women are entering bourgeois professions, intensifying competition here and contributing to an income structure where the intellectual worker can no longer independently provide for a family.

In the social sphere, a new type of marriage is added to the ones that already exist: the intellectually and economically independent woman is directly rooted in society and assumes obligations towards it, in which the man no longer shares. She represents only herself outwardly. The more opportunities are provided for her to satisfy her creative work drive outside the home, the less significant a role marriage may play in her life plan. Instead of adjusting her life to her marriage, she will now strive to adapt her marriage to a life that has shifted its focus outward.

This adaptation occurs amidst constant conflict between tradition and new life, but the mindset of the growing youth in these circles already contains an image of a mother whose hours not devoted to children are as unchanging as those of the father, who, just like the father, merely inquires about incidents in the children's room instead of experiencing them. Here, the tradition of the good mother and housewife is already being dismantled, and the shaping of marital form becomes freer from ties to values that do not align with one's own life destiny.

This marriage has not yet found its form, but its content is already discernible: it is an erotic companionship bond between equals, whose sole purpose can lie in the enhancement of life's value. If it does not fulfill this purpose, then it becomes futile for the spouses and for the children, for whom it can no longer secure the harmony of the environment – the only thing that non-residential parenthood can still offer their offspring. In reality, this marriage is already dissolved if it is no longer desired by even one spouse and if there is no one here for whom the formal maintenance of the marital bond through state authority would be necessary for protection.

Here, just like the man, the woman is not thrown out of a home that means the world to her by divorce; she doesn't lose her place of work and influence, nor her social status, and she can remain an unburdened mother despite an unhappy marriage – unless she prefers to entrust the children to a communal upbringing. With the end of this marriage, a dream of happiness comes to an end, but personal happiness is not a matter for governmental administration.

The bourgeois woman is only now entering the workforce – the proletarian housewife, that is, the wife of the wage proletariat exposed to all the whims of the market, has already tried to supplement the meagre earnings of her husband as early as the beginnings of capitalism. First, it was home-based work that brought her earning opportunities into the household, lending a semblance of small bourgeoisie to her marriage. Then came the factory, shaping her fate. The proletarian woman was torn from her home, yet the home continued to demand her fulfillment of all domestic duties.

The tremendous burden imposed on women by factory work was certainly alleviated by labour protection legislation, the eight-hour day, and the English Saturday, but where the earning wife is also a mother, her life is filled with haste and restlessness, from which she yearns to escape at any cost. For many women here, the privilege of being nothing more than a housewife and mother often becomes the substance of the boldest and most unattainable dreams!

The proletarian housewife, even where she is not a co-provider, does not suffer from the sense of inferiority that certainly played a role in the entry of bourgeois women into public life. The dignity of her contributions provides her with inner assurance, both to her husband and to the children who receive everything from her hands that the care for daily life can offer. She works to earn and assist her family, but when her strength no longer suffices or when her husband's earnings allow it, she becomes the 'woman of her own household'.

The woman in the small household forms a distinct type that appears associated with the 'past' and yet is produced by modern development. Modern industry creates a broad layer of highly skilled workers, whose wages are considered sufficient for family maintenance, not because they are high, but because they are higher than the average income of this class. The administrative tasks of the modern state and municipalities give rise to a numerous class of middle-level civil servants, whose household demands the entire labour force of the woman and seems to provide her protection from the accidents of life. And it is here that the woman thrives, giving all her mental and physical strength to the family, remaining in need of protection and dependent, while safeguarding and liberating others who cannot move forward without the crutch of marriage. She is much more bound to marriage than her spouse, and therefore, also weaker in relation to him. Her devotion to marriage creates rights and obligations, and here it applies: only one who joins with the free is truly free.

The unfolding of modern life creates conditions for the proletarian and semi-proletarian housewife, 'driving broad masses to seek refuge in small trade and the remaining branches of handicraft', thereby continuously generating the 'traditional' economic marriage. However, it also gives rise to new fields of work for women from proletarian and petit-bourgeois circles. The working woman here is no longer solely reliant on the laborious and monotonous work in the factory, in comparison to which even the most modest home must have seemed like a hoped-for bright future. The saleswoman in the department store, the office employee, the bank clerk are reluctant to trade the positions that offer advancement opportunities – prospects of trusted positions – and thereby ignite their professional ambition for the work in their own household, from which they already feel psychologically and physically detached after a few years spent in their profession. They no longer give up their employment and job willingly, without external pressure; they flee from marriage and from motherhood.

Their disillusionment with marriage arises from the feeling that a man, raised by a good mother and desiring to be further mothered, is not a suitable husband for a working woman. No housekeeper or educator can bestow the illusion of a good housewife and mother upon her. She realises that she must disappoint his marital hopes if she wishes to preserve her own personality. She tenaciously defends her right to an independent existence even within marriage. Being bolder than the bourgeois woman against the shackles of convention and more determined than the factory worker against the dual burden of employment and housework, she compels society to perceive the challenges of her marriage as a societal problem.

Marriage, fatefully binding man and woman to shared tasks, marriage that brings together individuals rooted in society and thereby independent beings, marriage that connects the woman to society only through the home or burdens the working woman with her small concerns – all of these are marriages of today. They differ not only in the degree of commitment of the two partners to the marriage, in the economic and social significance of marriage for the woman, in the degree of responsibility of the man towards the woman, but perhaps even more so in the extent of conflicts that modern employment and the dethroning of domestic management bring into the marriage. Across the broad spectrum ranging from the well-defined structure of the agricultural economic marriage to the loose marital arrangement of two intellectual workers, public servants, employees, the old bonds fade, new ones emerge, yielding to obligations and rights that become hollow and void, meaningful only for one partner here, for both partners there. Domestic management turns into household, into home, and around the home, a marriage arises that is pure will, sustained only through the will to fidelity.[1]

The occupational and social structure of modern society constitutes a fact that is well-known to every adult: the necessity for a variety of marital and family arrangements to emerge from it is not acknowledged by society, legislation, or unfortunately by many who willingly undertake an exhausting struggle to find a compromise between traditional forms and their own life circumstances. However, this lack of knowledge and unwillingness to see facilitates the enactment of marriage laws that correspond to a guild mentality, opposing the modern way of life, for some. It also makes it difficult for others to dispel the old ideology that confuses and hinders their quest for formation, even though it still fully corresponds to the social significance of marriage within other strata.

---

1 That these marriages, by their very nature, create lasting bonds, refer to Georg Simmel's *Sociology*, Leipzig 1908, page 583: 'For relationships that unfold between individuals correspond in them to a specific feeling directed towards the relationship, an interest, an impulse. If the relationship continues, then, in interaction with this continued existence, a particular feeling arises, or also: those originally established mental states metamorphose – often, if not always – into a distinct form that we call fidelity, as it were into a psychological reservoir or a form of totality or unity for the manifold interests, affections, binding motives; and across all the diversity of their origins, they assume a certain uniformity in the form of fidelity, which conceptually favours the enduring nature of this feeling'. Similar thoughts can also be found in the individual psychological work 'The Marriage of Today and Tomorrow' by Sophie Lazarsfeld, Munich 1927.

Appendix

Helene Bauer's Essays in *Der Kampf* in Chronological Order

Selbstbestimmung der Arbeit (Self-Determination of Labour) *1919*
Rudolf Gotscheids "Naturalabgabe" (Rudolf Gotscheids "Contribution in Kind") *1919*
Vermögensabgabe und Sozialisierung (Property Levy and Sozialisation) *1919*
"Der Wirtschaftsplan" ('The Economic Plan') *1919*
Zur Auslandspolitik des Bolschewismus (On the Foreign Policy of Boslhevism) *1919*
Internationale Voraussetzungen des Sozialismus (International Conditions for Socialism) *1919*
Aussprechen, was ist? (To Say, What is?) *1919*
An der Schwelle der neuen Zeit (On the Threshold of the New Time) *1919*
Sozialistische Bildungsfargen nach den Umsturz (Socialist Education After the Coup) *1919*
Aus den Problemen der Weltwirtschaft (From the Problems of the World Economy) *1919*
Kommunisten und Räterepublik (Communists and the Council Republic) *1920*
Der Kampf um auskömmliche Nahrung (The Struggle for Sufficient Food) *1920*
Zur Frage der proletarischen Agrarpolitik (On the Question of the Proletarian Agricultural Policy) *1921*
Sovietrussland und das ausländische Kapital (Soviet Russia and the Foreign Capital) *1921*
Herr Ottmar Spanns – Tischlein deck dich (Mr. Ottmar Spanns – table set yourself) *1922*
Die Interessenharmonie, der "gemeine Mann" und ein besserer Herr (The Harmony of Interests, the 'Common Man' and a Better Gentleman) *1923*
Theoretisches zur österreichischen Handelsbilanz vol. 1. (Theorietical Treatise on Austrian Trade Balance vol. 1.) *1923*
Geld, Sozialismus und Otto Neurath (Money, Socialism and Otto Neurath) *1923*
Sozialistische Wirtschaftsrechnung, vol. 9–10 (Socialist Economic Calculation, vol. 9–10) *1923*
Bankrott der Grenznutzentheorie (Bankruptcy of Marginal Utility Theory) *1924*
Der imperialistische Krieg (The Imperialist War) *1924*
Klassenkämpfe und Agrarreform in Polen (Class struggles and agrarian reform in Poland) *1924*
Cassels "wertfreie" Sozialökonomie (Cassels' "Value-Free" Social Economy) *1925*
Zur Theorie der Marktpreise bei Marx (On Theory of Market Prices by Marx) *1925*
Bürgerliche und Sozialistische Wirtschaftstheorie (Bourgeois and Socialist Economic Theory) *1926*
Parteien und Putsch in Polen (Political Parties and Coup in Poland) *1926*
Akkumulation, Kredit und Imperialismus (Accumulation, Credit, and Imperialism) *1927*

Der Imperialismus (Imperialism) *1927*
Ehe und soziale Schichtung (Marriage and Social Stratification) *1927*
Der Guburtenrückgang (Decline in the Birthrate) *1928*
Internationale Kapitalskonzentration und Lenin Katastrophentheorie des Imperialismus (International Concentration of Capital and Lenin's Theory of the Imperialism of Catastrophe) *1928*
Franz Oppenheimers Kritik des Marxismus (Franz Oppenheimer's Critique of Matxism) *1929*
Ein neuer Zusammenbruchstheoretiker (A New Breakdown Theorist) *1929*
Ein sozialistisches Lehrbuch (A Socialist Textbook) *1930*
Zu Weltwirtschaftskrise (On Crisis in World Economy) *1931*
Sozalismus in einem Lande (Socialism in One Country) *1931*
Die Fehlleitung des Kapitals (Misdirection of Capital) *1932*
Im Vierten Krisenjahr (In the Fourth Year of Crisis) *1932*
Konjunkturaufschwung und Faschismus (Economic Boom and Fascism) *1936*.

In *Neue Zeit*

Ein Beitrag zur Frage des landwirtschaftlichen Kleinbetriebs / von Helena Landau-Gumplowicz. – Die neue Zeit: Wochenschrift der deutschen Sozialdemokratie. 31.1912–1913, 2. Bd. (1913), H. 51, S. 957–65.
Zur Literatur über Polen – Die neue Zeit: Wochenschrift der deutschen Sozialdemokratie. 34.1915–1916, 1. Bd. (1915), H. 8, S. 249–52.

Books

Zur Entwicklung des Warenhandels in Österreich. 1905.

In Journal Bildungsarbeit

Die wirtschaftliche Voraussetzungen der Internationale, 10 (5): 33–4.

Bibliography

Adler, Max 1981, 'Der Krieg ist aus', in: *Ausgewählte Schriften*, Wien: Österreichischer Bundesverlag.

Althusser, Louis 1994 [1982], '*Le courant souterrain du matérialisme de la rencontre*', in: *Ècrits philosophiques et politiques, Tome I*, Paris: Èditions STOCK/IMEC.

Anderson, Bonnie S. and Judith P. Zinsser 1988, *Eine eigene Geschichte – Frauen in Europa*, Zürich: Schweizer Verlagshaus.

Ausch, Karl 1973, '*Genfer Sanierung und der 12. Februar 1934*', in *Österreich 1927 bis 1938. Protokoll des Symposiums in Wien 23. Bis 28. Oktober1972*, edited by Ludwig Jedlicka and Rudolf Neck, Wien: Verlag für Geschichte und Politik: 97–103.

Austerlitz, Friedrich 1919, '*Los von Wien!*', in: *Der Kampf*, 12, 9, 1919: 345–49.

Baier, Walter 2021, 'Introduction', in Otto Bauer *The Austrian Revolution*, edited by Walter Baier and Eric Canepa, New York: Haymarket.

Baran Paul and Paul Sweezy 1964, *Monopoly Capital*, New York: Monthly Review Press.

Bauer, Helene 1919 A, '*Rudolf Goldscheids „Naturalabgabe"*', *Der Kampf*, 12, 6, 1919: 270–3.

Bauer, Helene 1919 B, '*Vermögensabgabe und Sozialisierung*', *Der Kampf*, 12, 7, 1919: 291–4.

Bauer, Helene 1919 C, '*Der Wirtschaftsplan*', *Der Kampf*, 12,8, 1919: 341–2.

Bauer, Helene 1922, '*Herr Ottmar Spanns Tischlein deck dich*', *Der Kampf*, 15, 6, 1922: 187–92.

Bauer, Helene 1923 A, '*Geld, Sozialismus und Otto Neurath*', *Der Kampf*, 16, 5, 1923: 195–202.

Bauer, Helene 1923 B, *Die Interessenharmonie, der "gemeine Mann" und ein "besserer Herr". Arbeit und Wirtschaft. Organ der Gewerkschaftskommission, Arbeiterkammern und Betriebsräte Österreichs* 1 (1923): 589–92.

Bauer, Helene 1924 '*Bankrott der Grenzwerttheorie*', *Der Kampf*, 17, 3, 1924: 105–13.

Bauer, Helene 1924 A, '*Der imperialistische Krieg*', *Der Kampf*, 17, 10, 1924: 382–90.

Bauer, Helene 1925 A, '*Cassels wertfreie Sozialökonomie*', *Der Kampf*, 18, 3, 1925: 89–95.

Bauer, Helene 1925 B, '*Emil Lederer: Grundzüge der ökonomischen Theorie*', *Der Kampf*, 18, 7, 1925: 278–9.

Bauer, Helene 1926, '*Bürgerliche und sozialistische Wirtschaftstheorie*', *Der Kampf*, 19, 2, 1926: 63–8.

Bauer, Helene 1927 A, '*Der Imperialismus*', *Der Kampf* 20, 1, 1927: 7–12.

Bauer, Helene 1927 B, '*Akkumulation, Kredit und Imperialismus*', *Der Kampf* 20, 4, 1927: 173–8.

Bauer, Helene 1927 C, '*Die Ehe und die soziale Schichtung*', *Der Kampf* 20, 7, 1927: 319–24.

Bauer, Helene 1928, '*Internationale Kapitalskonzentration und leninistische Katastrophentheorie des Imperialismus*', *Der Kampf* 21, 8/9, 1928: 392–400.

Bauer, Helene 1929, *'Ein neuer Zusammenbruchstheoretiker'*, *Der Kampf*, 22, 6, 1929: 270–9.

Bauer, Helene 1931, *'Zur Weltwirtschaftskrise'*, *Der Kampf*, 24,3, 1931: 117–24.

Bauer, Helene 1932, *'Im vierten Krisenjahr'*, *Der Kampf*, 25,12, 1932: 493–9

Bauer, Helene 1936, *'Konjunktur Aufschwung des Faschismus'*, *Der Kampf*, 29, 12, 1936: 469–74.

Bauer, Otto 1919, *Der Weg zum Sozialismus*, Wien: Verlag Wiener Volksbuchhandlung.

Bauer, Otto 1920, *Bolschewismus oder Sozialdemokratie*, Wien: Verlag der Wiener Volksbuchhandlung.

Bauer, Otto 1931, *Protokoll der Sitzung des Verbandes der sozialdemokratischen Abgeordneten und Bundesräte vom 19, Juni 1931*, Archive des IGA Vienna.

Bauer, Otto 1956, *Einführung in die Volkswirtschaftslehre*, Wien: Verlag der Wiener Volksbuchhandlung.

Bauer, Otto 1978, *Werkausgabe*, Vol. 5, Wien: Europaverlag.

Bauer, Otto 1979, *Die alte und die neue Linke*, in Otto Bauer, *Werkausgabe*, Vol. 8. Wien: Europaverlag.

Bauer, Otto 1980, *Sozialismus und Wissenschaft*, in Otto Bauer, *Werkausgabe*, Wien: Europaverlag.

Bauer, Otto and Karl Kautsky 1995, Brief, 6, März 1919, in Herbert Steiner, *Die Österreichische Arbeiterbewegung und die Anschlußfrage*, Berlin: Akademieverlag.

Bauer, Otto 2020, *The Austrian Revolution*, edited by Walter Baier und Eric Canepa, Chicago IL: Haymarket Books.

Bauer, Otto 2021, *Der Aufstand der österreichischen Arbeiter. Seine Ursachen und seine Wirkung*, Vienna: ÖGB Verlag.

Bihl, Wolfdieter 1989, *Von der Donaumonarchie zur Zweiten Republik. Daten zur österreichischen Geschichte seit 1867*, Wien: Böhlau Studienbücher.

Blythe, Mark 2013, *Austerity: The History of a Dangerous Idea*, Oxford: Oxford University Press.

Braunthal, Julius 1961, *Otto Bauer: Eine Auswahl aus seinem Lebenswerk*, Vienna: Verlag der Wiener Volksbuchhandlung.

Caldwell, Bruce 2004, *Hayek's Challenge: An Intellectual Biography of F.A. Hayek*, Chicago IL, University of Chicago Press.

Cassel, Gustav 1967, *The Theory of Social Economy*, Reprints of Economic Classics, New York: Augustus M. Kelley Publishers.

Chaloupek, Günther. K 1990, 'The Austrian Debate on Economic Calculation in a Socialist Economy', *History of Political Economy*, 22, 4, (1990): 659–75.

Chaloupek, Günther. K 2016, *Zwischen Inflation, Staatsbankrott und Sozialisierung: Schumpeter im Malstrom der Wirtschaftspolitik der Republik Deutsch-Österreich*, Referat beim Symposium 'Josef Schumpeter Heute' October, 14. 2016. http://www.chaloupek.eu/en/wp-content/uploads/Schumpeter-2.pdf

Goldscheid, Rudolf 1964, 'A sociological approach to problems of public finance', in *Classics in Theory of Public Finance*, edited by R.A. Musgrave and A.T. Peacock, London: Macmillan for the International Economic Association: 202–13.

Hauch, Gabriella 1995, Vom Frauenstandpunkt aus. Frauen im Parlament 1919–1933, *Studien zur Gesellschafts- und Kulturgeschichte 7* – Veröffentlichungen des Ludwig-Bolzmann-Institut für die Geschichte der ArbeiterInnenbewegung.

Hayek, Friedrich. A 1978, *Interview with Leo Rosten*. https://ia801407.us.archive.org/18/items/nobelprizewinninoohaye/nobelprizewinninoohaye.pdf

Hayek, Friedrich. A 1994, *Hayek on Hayek: An Autobiographical Dialogue*, edited by S. Kresge & L. Wenar, Chicago IL: University of Chicago Press.

Hauptmann, Hans 1971, *Die verlorene Räterepublik. Am Beispiel der Kommunistischen Partei Deutschösterreichs*, Wien: Europaverlag.

Helling, Ingeborg K 1988, '*Strömungen des methodologischen Individualismus – Alfred Schütz, Felix Kaufmann und der Mises-Kreis*', in *Geschichte der Österreichischen Soziologie – Konstituierung, Entwicklung und europäische Bezüge*, edited by Josef Langer, Wien: Verlag für Gesellschaftskritik.

Hirsch, Bettina 1927, '*Hausfrau und Einküchehaus. Schlussbetrachtung*', in *Das kleine Blatt*, 24, September 1927.

Hülsmann, Jörg G. 2007, *Mises: The Last Knight of Liberalism*, Auburn AL: Ludwig von Mises Institute.

Internationale Tagung der Historiker der Arbeiterbewegung – XIV Linzer Konferenz 1978, Wien: Europa Verlag, 1980.

Karnute 1919, *Wie soll sich Kärnten orientieren?*, in *Grazer Tagblatt*, 16, Juli 1919. S. 1–2.

Kautsky, Karl 1914, '*Der Imperialismus*', *Die Neue Zeit*, 2, 21, September, 11. 1914.

Kelsen, Hans 1923, *Österreichiches Staatsrecht*, Tübingen: Mohr.

Kerekes, Lajos 1975, '*Die wirtschaftliche und soziale Lage Österreichs nach dem Zerfall der Doppelmonarchie*', *Acta Historica Academiae Scientiarum Hungaricae*, Budapest: Institute of History, Research Centre for the Humanities, Hungarian Academy of Sciences, 21, 3/4 (1975): 349–63.

King, John E. 2019, *The Alternative Austrian Economics*, Glos: Edward Elgar Publishing.

Kulka, Leopoldine 1910, Auguste Flickert, in *Neues Frauenleben*, Juli 1910.

Landau, Helene 1906, *Die Entwicklung des Warenhandels in Österreich. Ein Beitrag zur Wirtschaftspolitik des Absolutismus*, Wien und Leipzig: Braumüller.

Landau, Helene 1913, *Wobec nowych traktatów handlowych*, Kraków.

Lange Helene and Gertrud Bäumer 1902, *Der Stand der Frauenbildung in Österreich*, Österreichische Nationalbibliothek, Wien.

Lanzer, Wanda 1950, *Letter to Marianne Polack*, Helene Bauer Archive 19/41, Verein für Geschichte der Arbeiterbewegung, Aug. 20, 1950.

Larise, Dunja 2007, *Würfelspiel des Zufalls – Aleatorischer Materialismus – Ein politisch-philosophisches Projekt von Louis Althusser*, Marburg: Tectum.

Leichter, Otto 1970, *Otto Bauer: Tragödie oder Triumph*, Wien-Frankfurt-Zürich: Europaverlag.

Linzer Programm der Sozialistischen Arbeiterpartei Deutschösterreichs von Nov, 3th 1926, https://www.marxists.org/deutsch/geschichte/oesterreich/spoe/1926/linzerprog.htm

Lösch, Andrea 1985, *Probleme der Frauenarbeit in Österreich 1918–1920. Sozialpolitische Maßnahmen zur Ausgliederung von Frauen aus der Erwerbsarbeit*, Wien: Diplomarbeit.

Luxemburg, Rosa 1913, *Die Akkumulation des Kapitals. Ein Beitrag zur ökonomischen Theorie des Imperialismus*, Berlin: Buchhandlung Vorwärts Paul Singer GmbH.

Magaziner, Alfred 1979, *Helene Bauer – Eine Schönheit mit Verstand*, in Alfred Magaziner, *Die Vorkämpfer – Aus der Geschichte der Arbeiterbewegung*, Wien – München – Zürich: Europaverlag.

Mayer, Hans 1900, *'Zurechnung'*, in *Handwörterbuch der Staatswissenschaften*, edited by L. Elster, A. Weber und F. Wiesel, Jena: Verlag von Gustav Fischer.

Mises, Ludwig 1920, *Wirtschaftsrechnung im sozialistischen Gemeinwesen*, Wien, *Archiv für Sozialwissenschaften* 47, 1920: 86–121.

Mises, Ludwig 1922, *Die Gemeinwirtschaft, Untersuchungen über den Sozialismus*, Jena: Gustav Fischer Verlag.

Mises, Ludwig 1925, *Antimarxismus*, *Weltwirtschaftliches Archiv* 21, (1925).

Mises, Ludwig 1927, *Liberalismus*, Jena: Verlag von Gustav Fischer.

Mises, Ludwig 1933, *Grundprobleme der Nationalökonomie*, Jena: Verlag von Gustav Fischer.

Mises, Ludwig 1998, *Human Action – A Treatise on Economics*, Auburn, AL: Ludwig von Mises Institute.

Mises, Ludwig 1927, *Liberalism – The Classical Tradition*, Indianapolis: Liberty Fund.

Mises, Ludwig 1978, Memories – *With an Introduction by Friedrich August Hayek*, Stuttgart-New York: Gustav Fisher.

Moszkowska, Natalie 1931, '*Strukturwandel des Kapitalismus*' – *Ein Beitrag zum Krisenproblem, Der Kampf*, 24, 1, 1931: 30–7. *Neue Freie Presse*, November, 12. 1918.

Neurath, Otto 1928, *Lebensgestaltung und Klassenkampf*, Berlin: E. Laubische Verlagsbuchhandlung G.m.b.H.

Obituaries on Helene Bauer, Unpublished, Archive Helene Bauer 19/41, Verein für Geschichte der Arbeiterbewegung, Vienna.

Olechowsky, Thomas; Tamara Echs, and Kamila Staudigl-Ciechowicz (2014). *Die Wiener Rechts – und Staatwissenschaftliche Fakultät 1918–1938*, Wien: Vienna University Press.

Peukert, Helge 2023, *Rudolf Goldschied: Finanzsoziologie des Steuerstaates*, Marburg: Metropolis.

Polanyi, Karl 1922, *Sozialistische Rechnungslegung*, Wien, *Archiv für Sozialwissenschaft und Sozialpolitik* 47, 2, 1922: 377–93.

Renner, Karl 1924, *Die Wirtschaft als Gesamtprozess und die Sozialisierung*, Berlin: J.H.W. Dietz Nachfolger.

Renner, Karl 1931, *Protokoll des sozialdemokratischen Parteitages*, abgehalten vom 13. Bis 15. November 1931 in Graz. Archive des IGA, Wien.

Robinson, M. 1942, *Obituary for Helene Bauer*, Helene Bauer Archive 19/41, Verein für die Geschichte der Arbeiterbewegung, Vienna.

Rotschild, Kurt 1947, 'Price Theory and Oligopoly', *Economic Journal*, 57, 227, September: 299–320.

Röder, Werner und Herbert A. Strauss 1999, *Biografisches Handbuch der deutschsprachigen Emigration*, München: K.G. Saur.

Schlesinger, Therese 1921, 'Die Frauen und die Revolution', *Der Kampf*, 14, 2/3, 1921: 73–6.

Schlesinger, Therese 1925, *Frauenarbeit und proletarische Lebenshaltung*, in *Arbeiter-Zeitung*, 8. Februar 1925.

Schneider, Karin 2008, *Historische Bezüge von frauen- und genderpolitischen Positionen im Austromarxismus*, in *Otto Bauer und der Austromarxismus*, edited bv Walter Baier, Lisbeth N. Trallori and Derek Weber, Berlin: Karl Dietz Verlag.

Schröder, Hans-Cristoph 1973, *Sozialistische Imperialismusdeutung – Studien zu ihrer Geschichte*, Göttingen: Vadenhoeck und Ruprecht.

Schülz, Alfred 1960, *Der sinnhafte Aufbau der sozialen Welt*, Wien: Springer Verlag.

Schumpeter, Joseph 1918, *Die Krise des Steuerstaates*, Graz und Leipzig: Verlag Leuschner & Lubensky.

Schumpeter, Joseph 1919, *Zur Soziologie des Imperialismus, Archiv für Sozialwissenschaft und Sozialpolitik*, Tübingen: J.C.B. Mohr, 46 (1919): 1–39.

Schumpeter, Joseph 1949, *The Theory of Economic Development: An Inquiry into Profits, Capital, Credit, Interest and the Business Cycle*, Cambridge, Massachusetts: Harvard Univesity Press.

Schumpeter, Joseph 1992, *Politische Reden*, edited by Seidl Christian and Wolfgang F. Stolper, Tübingen: J.C.B. Mohr.

Simon, Walter 1984, *Österreich 1918–1938. Ideologien und Politik*, Wien: Hermann Böhlaus Nachf. Verlag.

Sozialdemokratische Arbeiterpartei Österreichs 1926, "Linzer Programm".

Stadler, Karl 1968, *Hypothek auf die Zukunft. Die Entstehung der österreichischen Republik 1918–1921*, Wien: Europa Verlag.

Steiner, Herbert 1997, *Käthe Leichter: Leben, Werk und Sterben einer Österreichischen Sozialdemokratin*, Wien: Ibera & Molden Verlag.

Stockhammer, Engelbert (forthcoming 2024) Another Austrian School, *Historical Materialism Journal Special Edition*, edited by Dunja Larise and Walter Baier.

Sturmthal, Adolf 1937, *Die große Krise*, Zürich: Oprecht.

Tanenhaus, Sam 1997, *Whittaker Chambers: A Biography*, New York: Random House.

Tasca, Angelo 1965, *Nascita e avvento del fascismo: L'Italia dal 1918 al 1922*, Torino: Laterza.

Thalheimer, August 1928, *Über den Faschismus*, in *Faschismus und Kapitalismus – Theorien über die sozialen Ursprünge und Funktion des Faschismus*, edited by Abendroth Wolfgang, Leipzig: EVA Verlag.

Weber, Fritz 1986, *'Der kalte Krieg in der SPÖ. Koalitionswächter, Pragmatiker und revolutionäre Sozialisten 1945–1950'*, *Österreichische Texte zur Gesellschaftskritik*, 25, Wien: Verlag der Postgewerkschaft.

Weisensteiner, Friedrich 1990, *Der ungeliebte Staat – Österreich zwischen 1918–1938*, Wien: Österreichischer Bundesverlag.

West, Franz 1934, *Lehrheft zur Geschichte der österreichischen Arbeiterbewegung*, vom 15. Juli 1927 bis zum 12. Februar 1934, Wien.

Winkler, Ernst 1967, Helene Bauers letzte Lebenstage. In: *Auf den Zinnen der Partei. Ausgewählte Schriften*, Wiener Neustadt: Druck- und Verlagsanstalt Gutenberg.

Zeisl, Franz 1930, *Ein Einwand gegen die Marxsche Wertlehre*, *Der Kampf*, 23,8, 1930: 391–4.

Index

www.ingramcontent.com/pod-product-compliance
Lightning Source LLC
LaVergne TN
LVHW012056160826
845678LV00014B/2851

9798888908884